Edgar Fawcett

Fantasy and passion

Edgar Fawcett

Fantasy and passion

ISBN/EAN: 9783337810276

Printed in Europe, USA, Canada, Australia, Japan

Cover: Foto ©ninafisch / pixelio.de

More available books at **www.hansebooks.com**

Fantasy and Passion.

BY

EDGAR FAWCETT.

BOSTON:
ROBERTS BROTHERS.
1878.

Copyright,
BY ROBERTS BROTHERS.
1878.

Cambridge:
Press of John Wilson and Son.

TO

THOMAS BAILEY ALDRICH,

WITH ESTEEM AND ADMIRATION.

CONTENTS.

I. MINORCHORDS.

	PAGE
SEA-GULLS	3
REVERIE	4
AN INTERIOR	5
AN OLD TEA-CUP	6
AFFINITIES	7
TO THE EVENING STAR	9
A HUMMING-BIRD	10
TO AN ORIOLE	11
HEAT-LIGHTNING	11
CLOUDS	13
A STRAGGLER	14
WATER-LILIES	16
FANTAISIE DE PRINTEMPS	17
ANALOGIES	18
RARITY	20
VIOLETS IN WINTER	21
IMMORTELLES	22
TO A TEA-ROSE	23
WILD ROSES	24
A TUBEROSE	25

CONTENTS.

	PAGE
IVY	26
HEMLOCKS	28
THE ACORN	29
FERNS	30
MOSS	31
LEAVES	32
CLOVER	33
GRAPES	34
A TOAD	36
WEEDS	37
A BAT	38
BOX	39
DEW	41
FIREFLIES	42
FOUR DAYS	43

II. VOICES AND VISIONS.

THE HOUSE ON THE HILL	49
FIDELITAS	57
ADORATION	59
IF TRULY	63
DARKNESS	64
HIS CHILD	65
SELF-DECEPTION	67
CHIAROSCURO	68
A BIRD OF PASSAGE	69
A LEAVE-TAKING	70

CONTENTS.

	PAGE
VESTA	71
ONE NIGHT IN SEVILLE	72
BARCAROLLE	73
CRADLE-SONG	75
ONE MAY NIGHT	77
FORGETFULNESS	78
SOUVENIR	80
THE MEETING	81
D'OUTRE MORT	82
FROM SHADOWLAND	83
PEST	85
WINE	86
TO-MORROW	88
DEGREE	89
THE ATONEMENT	90
TIGER TO TIGRESS	91
JAEL	93
VIOLANTE	97
MOZART'S REQUIEM	105
BEHIND HISTORY	108
THE STATUETTE	110
INDIVIDUALITY	111
ORDER	113
CONCEPTION	114
FAME	115
CRITICISM	117
ATTAINMENT	118
A KING	119

	PAGE
WINDS	120
THE COMET	122
THE ICEBERG	124
PERSPECTIVES	127
THE MOON IN THE CITY	128
FIRE	129
DECAY	130
WASTE	131
DECORATION DAY	132
CUSTER	134
CUBA	135
ALBERT F. WEBSTER, JR.	136
TO EDWIN BOOTH	138
THE SCHOLAR'S SWEETHEART	139
LA BELLE HÉLÈNE	141
GENTLEMAN JO	144
PIPES AND BEER	147
TO AN OLD STREET-LAMP	150
A BARNYARD ECLOGUE	153

III. SONNETS.

ART	161
GENIUS	162
SLEEP	163
TO ——	164
THE CITY	165
KINDLINESS	166

CONTENTS.

	PAGE
COMMONPLACES	167
CITY WINDOWS	168
A THISTLE	169
MAPLES	170
A COBWEB	171
AN OCTOBER DAY	172
A WILLOW-TREE	173
THISTLEDOWN	174
FABRICS:	
I. VELVET	175
II. SATIN	176
III. BROCADE	177
THE OLD MIRROR	178
EARTHQUAKE	179
TO F. S. S.	180
MEDUSA	181
ANTIPODES:	
I. POE	182
II. WHITTIER	183
CAMEOS:	
I. THACKERAY	184
II. DICKENS	185
III. KEATS	186
IV. DUMAS, *Père*	187
V. HANS CHRISTIAN ANDERSEN	188
VI. HERBERT SPENCER	189
VII. GUSTAVE DORÉ	190
VIII. BAUDELAIRE	191

I.

MINORCHORDS.

FANTASY AND PASSION.

SEA-GULLS.

THE salt sea-wind is a merry-maker,
   Rippling the wild bluff's daisied reach;
The quick surf glides from the arching breaker
   And foams on the tawny beach.

Out where the long reef glooms and glances
   And tosses sunward its diamond rains,
Morn has pierced with her golden lances
   The dizzy light-house panes.

Gladdened by sounds of infinite surges,
   Heedless what billow or gale may do,
The white gulls float where the ocean-verges
   Blend with a glimmer of blue.

I watch how the curtaining vapor settles
   Dim on their tireless plumes far-borne,
Till faint they gleam as a blossom's petals
   Blown through the spacious morn!

REVERIE.

BELOW the headland, with its cedar plumes,
    A lapse of spacious water twinkles keen;
An ever-shifting play of gleams and glooms,
    And flashes of clear green.

The sumach's garnet pennons, where I lie,
    Are mingled with the tansy's faded gold;
Fleet hawks are screaming in the light-blue sky
    And fleet airs rushing cold.

The plump peach steals the dying rose's red;
    The yellow pippin ripens to its fall;
The dusty grapes, to purple fulness fed,
    Droop from the garden-wall.

And yet where rainbow foliage crowns the swamp,
    I hear in dreams an April robin sing,
And memory, amid this Autumn pomp,
    Strays with the ghost of Spring!

AN INTERIOR.

(After Willems.)

A CHAMBER where the wainscot woods
Are rich with dark shapes, odd of mold,
And where the time-touched arras hangs
In blendings of blue, green, and gold.

And dimly pictured, gleam the walls,
With here bluff huntsmen, all at tryst;
Here mounted knights; a falcon, here,
Wide-winged upon a lady's wrist.

But also the quaint chamber holds
A living lady, large and fair,
In luminous satin whitely clad,
With mild pearls in her auburn hair.

Near a low table doth she sit,
Whose thick stiff cloth, of massive size,
Wears in its mossy woof what seem
A hundred splendid tangled dyes.

There fruits in luscious color glow,
All that the daintiest whim could ask,
And garnet wine that brightly fills
A frail fantastic crystal flask.

And crouching at her feet, a hound,
Lean, sleek, and pale-gray like a dove,
Whines wistfully, and seeks her face
With starry eyes that look their love.

AN OLD TEA-CUP.

FRAIL dainty toy that time so gently saves
    To float unshattered on its wasteful waves,

And reach, through storms of ruin and dismay,
Hands that uplift thee lovingly to-day,

Good thanks for sparing from oblivion dim
These painted dames who beam about thy brim !

The lips that touched thee once have lent an art
To murmur memories through my dreaming heart !

I see rich chambers draped with pink and gold,
Where sportive cherubs gleam in gilded mold ;

Where thick on cabinet and on mantel range
Rare gaudy Chinese monsters, grim and strange ;

Where lights from massive candelabra fall
On satined prince and scarlet cardinal ;

Where blooming ladies gayly group, arrayed
In fleecy wig, rouge, patch, and stiff brocade ;

And where the royal Louis, suave and bland,
Bows low to kiss one jewel-burdened hand ! . . .

Ah, me ! those merry courtiers and their King
No more with mirth make Trianon's alleys ring ;

His plumes no more the sworded gallant airs
In statued shrubbery and on marble stairs ;

And lovely laughing ladies move no more
Down fountained court or sculptured corridor!

And thou, poor cup, art loyal to thy past,
And sick of change, the cold iconoclast!

But since no longer those dear hours exist,
Pictured patrician, bright legitimist,

Then, if benignant aid be not in vain
To soothe the longings of thy lonely pain,

Oh, learn that shortly thou shalt treasured be
By one whose beauty is so sweet to see,

Her dazzling charms might thrill with envy pure
The shapeless dust that once was Pompadour!

AFFINITIES.

I.

SPEEDING across blank wastes of lonely snow
    From your pale palace, reared with wild device
    In a wild shadowy land of Arctic ice,
O North-wind, bitter North-wind, whither do you blow?

"Southward to find my tender languid love,
Who drowses in a clime of tropic haze,
Where, through the heavy-odored stagnant nights,
Great mellow fervid stars beam out above,
And where one sees, through sultry golden days,
The mighty Indian temples rear proud heights
And the rich-crested palm her green plume raise!

And I, the spirit strong to wreck and kill,
I, the stern North-wind, terrible to chill,
When her warm kisses through these cold lips
 thrill,
I have no will that is not her sweet will!"

II.

Bearing to lavish leaves your cadence low,
 From far off indolent lands of bloomful ease,
 Of gaudy birds and iridescent seas,
O South-wind, fragrant South-wind, whither do you
 blow?

"Northward to find my cruel white-limbed love,
Who dwells where all strange polar glories blaze;
Where, through the scintillant-starred long-lasting
 nights,
Auroral splendors up the dark heaven move,
And where one sees, through scant-lit freezing days,
Colossal ice-plinths, full of emerald lights,
House the huge walrus in their crystal maze!
 And I, the spirit whom all soft dreams fill,
 I, the bland South-wind, that can work no ill,
 When her cold kisses through these warm lips
  thrill,
 My life grows her life, and my will her will!"

TO THE EVENING STAR.

AGAIN, pale noiseless prophetess of night,
    I watch you dawn, your immemorial way,
And watch again your calm immaculate light
    Beam wistful on the dying smile of day!

Star wherewith dusk so chastely is impearled,
    If that you live for love indeed be true,
This yearning sorrowing sinful weary world
    Hath deep unutterable need of you!

Does Love in truth make your white bloom his own
    And thrill to blander gleams your luminous breast,
Meek silver lily, blossoming all alone
    In those dim flowerless meadows of the West?

Aloof your glimmering kindred burn and beat,
    High up in boundless quietudes of space,
And gazing on their dark domain, we meet
    The cold and awful infinite face to face!

But you are rich with radiance more divine,
    And pulsing as with balmiest pity's birth,
And tenderer, like a star not proud to shine,
    And lowlier, like a star that loves the earth!

And I, who watch your splendors quivering clear,
    Dream, ere from heavenly distance you depart,
Of some invisible mercy's falling tear,
    Of some invisible mercy's throbbing heart!

A HUMMING-BIRD.

WHEN the mild gold stars flower out,
   As the summer gloaming goes,
A dim shape quivers about
   Some sweet rich heart of a rose.

If you watch its fluttering poise,
   From palpitant wings will steal
A hum like the eerie noise
   Of an elfin spinning-wheel !

And then from the shape's vague sheen,
   Quick lustres of blue will float,
That melt in luminous green
   Round a glimmer of ruby throat !

But fleetly across the gloom
   This tremulous shape will dart,
While searching for some fresh bloom,
   To quiver about its heart.

Then you, by thoughts of it stirred,
   Will dreamily question them:
"Is it a gem, half bird,
   Or is it a bird, half gem?"

TO AN ORIOLE.

HOW falls it, oriole, thou hast come to fly
In tropic splendor through our Northern sky?

At some glad moment was it nature's choice
To dower a scrap of sunset with a voice?

Or did some orange tulip, flaked with black,
In some forgotten garden, ages back,

Yearning toward Heaven until its wish was heard,
Desire unspeakably to be a bird?

HEAT-LIGHTNING.

THE land is bathed in drowsy light,
And breezes move, with drowsy sigh,
From out that primrose West where now
The long day takes so long to die!

I watch the deepening dusk, I watch,
With soul to languid fancies given,
Night close the starry flowers on earth
And ope the flowerlike stars in heaven!

Not seen with more than transient look
If random glances near it stray,
Huge in the hueless East there hangs
One rounded cloud of stagnant gray.

The moments pass; a rapid bat
Traces black zigzags on the sky;
A beetle, bringing us his deep
Basso profundo, journeys by.

Down in the dim swamp, firefly throngs
A brilliant soundless revel keep,
As though beneath their radiant rain
Another Danaë slept her sleep!

The mild night grows; through meadowed ways
The globing dew makes odor sweet,
And slowly now, in that dark cloud,
A pulse of gold begins to beat!

With fitful brightenings, brief to last,
The tender flashes come and fly,
Each winning forth from vapory depths
A dreamy picture, rich of dye.

Drenched to its core with gentle fire,
The cloud, at every mellowing change,
Shows tranquil lakes and lovely vales
And massive mountains, range on range!

And standing in the summer gloom,
With placid rapture I behold
These luminous Andes of the air,
These ghostly Switzerlands of gold!

CLOUDS.

WHAT change with happiest thrill my pulse may start,
    Of all the unnumbered changes that I view
In these brief-loitering moods of heaven's deep heart,
    These tireless pilgrims of the buoyant blue?

Is it when drowsily through halcyon air
    They float in pillowy fleeces chaste as snow?
Or when against the horizon they loom fair,
    In towering Alpine peak and pale plateau?

Is it when shadowy as the vaguest dream
    Their pearly gossamers film the skies afar?
Or when like isles in quiet seas they gleam,
    Purple below the tremulous evening star?

Or yet when beauteous dawn, with rosy speed,
    Sunders their drapery where it darkly falls?
Or when from earth to sunset lands they lead,
    As stately stairways to imperial halls?

Or when like scales on fabulous dolphins' backs,
    They fleck with loveliest color evening gray?
Or when they move in grim tempestuous wracks,
    And through them javelins of hot lightning play?

Ah, no! whatever of joy such changes wake,
　That change above all others my soul sets,
Of when beneath some full-globed moon they make
　On sapphire calms their ghostly silhouettes!

For then, as through this dubious gloom they stray,
　Spirits they seem, with garments fluttering white,
Whose noiseless feet, in some miraculous way,
　Walk the great awful emptiness of the night!

A STRAGGLER.

I LEFT the throng whose laughter made
　That wide old woodland echo clear,
While forth they spread, in breezy shade,
　Their plethoric hamperfuls of cheer.

Along a dark moss-misted plank
　My way in dreamy mood I took,
And crossed, from balmy bank to bank,
　The impetuous silver of the brook.

And wandering on, at last I found
　A shadowy tranquil gladelike place,
Full of mellifluous leafy sound,
　While midmost of its grassy space

A lump of rugged granite gleamed,
　A tawny-lichened ledge of gray,
And up among the boughs there beamed
　One blue delicious glimpse of day!

In fitful faintness on my ear
   The picnic's lightsome laughter fell,
And softly while I lingered here,
   Sweet fancy bound me with a spell!

In some bland clime across the seas
   Those merry tones I seem to mark,
While dame and gallant roamed at ease
   The pathways of some stately park.

And in that glimpse of amethyst air
   I seemed to watch, with musing eye,
The rich blue fragment, fresh and fair,
   Of some dead summer's morning sky!

And that rough mass of granite, too,
   From graceless outlines gently waned,
And took the sculptured shape and hue
   Of dull old marble, deeply stained.

And then (most beauteous change of all!)
   Strown o'er its mottled slab lay low
A glove, a lute, a silken shawl,
   A vellum-bound Boccaccio!

WATER-LILIES.

UP in the loftier leafage, dense and dim,
    Of pines that slope to meet the lifeless pool,
And with still spicy coverts clothe its rim,
    The silvery fitful breeze comes fluting cool;
But rarely does it steal to this grave spot,
Dank with foul mire and rank with woody rot.

From half-sunk logs the sluggish turtles peer,
    The flabby emerald bull-frogs leap and pause;
The erratic dragon-flies float there and here,
    With rosy flashes in their wings of gauze;
And now a snake its sinuous way will thread,
With flickering tongue and small dark lifted head.

But out upon the central pool there blow
    The lily-legions these dull waters hold,
With hollowed petals dropping curves of snow
    Back from large fragrant stars of mossy gold,
All gleaming stainless on the unbroken sheen
Of heart-shaped leaves, in blended bronze and green.

And as I watch them, in serene array,
    And muse, while scenting their delicious balm,
Of how they burst from soilure and decay
    In taintlessness of alabaster calm,
And blossoming from this grim half-stagnant lake,
What sweet pure incongruity they make,

I dream of gloomy souls within whose deeps
    Crawls many a cold uncanny reptile thought;

Where black hate lurks and torpid envy sleeps,
  And yet wherein some saving grace has wrought
Some heavenly touch that all their darkness dowers
With the chaste charm of these immaculate flowers!

FANTAISIE DE PRINTEMPS.

IN the aisles of the orchard fair blossoms are drifting,
    The white petals drop one by one,
And the tulip's pale stalk from the garden is lifting
    A goblet of gems to the sun!

Come ramble awhile through this exquisite weather
    Of days that are fleet to pass,
When the stem of the willow shoots out a green feather,
    And buttercups burn in the grass!

When, pushing the soil from her bonny pink shoulders,
    The clover glides forth to the world,
And the fresh mosses gleam on the gray rugged boulders,
    With delicate May-dew impearled!

The brook in the pasture has hidden its pebbles,
    Full-flooded with April rain,
And listen, my love, to the silvery trebles
    That ring from the blossoming lane!

What vows to their sweethearts the gay robins utter!
    No marvel such wooers are heard!
Heigh ho! how the bosoms that scorn us would flutter,
    If man could make love like a bird!

ANALOGIES.

I LOUNGE against my garden gate;
   On one side heaven the sun hangs low;
Down one side crawls the exhausted storm
   That flashed and crashed an hour ago.
I lounge and see, with musing eye,
Two roses and a butterfly.

One is a sumptuous languid rose
   That bows its heavy lovely head,
While each fresh petal's velvet curve
   Burns with the same deep drowsy red;
Circe, her subtle self (who knows?)
Plotting new sorceries in a rose!

One is a pale pure bloom, with leaves
   Like satin in their lustres mild,
Half-closed, and faintlier flushed than looks
   The chaste palm of a little child;
Or pink as some late sunsets are,
That yearn to feel the evening star!

The butterfly's quick-quivering wings
   Wear each the blendings of such hues
As lurk in some old tapestry's
   Dim turmoil of golds, crimsons, blues;
Wings where dull smoldering color lies,
Lit richly with two peacock-eyes!

I watch this satrap of the air,
   Whose gorgeous rule hath such brief term,
This pirate of a floral sea,
   This beauteous burlesque of a worm,
In flower-like plumes, in bird-like power,
Kinned equally with bird or flower!

He cannot leave the great red rose;
   He flutters near her, loath to part
From all the fragrant charm which girds
   This blood-drop warm from summer's heart!
But on the pale rose, glimmering near,
The rain has left one radiant tear!

RARITY.

IN dreams I found a wondrous land,
    Radiant with roses on each hand.

No grasses, trees, nor shrubs were there,
But roses blossoming everywhere!

Great velvet-petalled blooms were these;
Red millions trembled in each breeze!

They swept toward the horizon's verge
In many a splendid ample surge;

They spread on all sides one intense
Monotony of magnificence! . . .

Then suddenly, where my pathway ran,
Loomed the vague presence of a man.

And in his clasp, with strange delight,
I saw one daisy, glimmering white!

Such daisies bloom, in slender sprays,
By throngs among June's meadowed ways.

Yet all my soul, at this weird hour,
Leaned out to that one simple flower!

For chastely, delicately fair,
And better still, supremely rare,

It wore a pastoral charm so sweet,
This lovely lissome marguerite,

That seeing it was like dear repose
To me, whose whole heart loathed a rose!

VIOLETS IN WINTER.

WHILE now the desolate lands are blank with snow,
      How sweet it is to know
Fierce winter dared by fragile foes like you,
Fresh beauteous lives that ever win the grace
      Of bathing each pure face
Mysteriously in heaven's own deeps of tender blue!

As the asters breathe of Autumn, so you bring
      Bland memories of new Spring,
And while your faint delicious balm one meets,
His spirit steals down blossoming orchard-ways,
      By warbling brooks he strays,
Or moves through calm campagnas of pale marguerites!

I know not where, mild flowers, I know not whence
      Is the dear difference
Between your blooms and many a one that blows!
Ah! delicate personality unknown,
      Ye are yourselves alone!
What is it makes the star a star, the rose a rose?

But in your chaste hearts Nature surely sets,
      Exquisite violets,
Meekness and lowlihead all traits above,
And seems through your soft faces to have smiled
      Like some young white-souled child,
Whose touch is benediction and whose looks are love!

IMMORTELLES.

JUST as when summer laughed they linger yet,
    Here in my chamber while the world is cold,
Their pale-gold brittle petals primly set
    About dry brittle hearts of deeper gold.

Is it but fancy that an aching need
    Lives in the wan inanimate looks they lift,
And that Tithonus-like they dumbly plead
    The awful goddess to revoke her gift?

Yes, if I read their joyless calm aright,
    Mere immortality can ill repay
This sluggish veto on corruption's blight,
    This dull and charmless challenge to decay!

For surely these are flowers that well might sleep
    Near Stygian waves and shiver in the breath
Of long disconsolate breezes when they sweep
    Out from the dreamy meadowlands of death!

Ah! where in this white urn they dimly smile,
    Full oft, I doubt not, each poor bloom has sighed
To have been some odorous radiance that erewhile
    Divinely was a rose, although it died!

TO A TEA-ROSE.

DEEP-FOLDED flower, for me your race
    Bears what no kindred blooms have borne
        That gleam in memory's vistas, —
A charm, a chastity, a grace
    The loveliest roses have not worn,
        Of all your lovely sisters!

Half tinged like some dim-yellow peach,
    Half like a shell's pink inward whorl
        That sighs its sea-home after,
Your creamy oval bud lets each
    Pale outer petal backward curl,
        Like a young child's lip in laughter!

And yet no mirthful trace we see;
    Rather the grave serene repose
        Of gentlest resignation;
So that you sometimes seem to be
    (If one might say it of a rose)
        In pensive meditation!

Ah! how may earthly words express
    This placid sadness round you cast,
        Delicate, vague, unspoken?
As though . . . . some red progenitress,
    In some old garden of the past,
        Had had her young heart broken!

WILD ROSES.

ON long serene midsummer days
   Of ripening fruit and yellowed grain,
How sweetly, by dim woodland ways,
   In tangled hedge or leafy lane,
Fair wild-rose thickets, you unfold
Those pale pink stars with hearts of gold!

Your sleek patrician sisters dwell
   On lawns where gleams the shrub's trim bosk,
In terraced gardens, tended well,
   Near pebbled walk and quaint kiosk.
In costliest urns their colors rest;
They beam on beauty's fragrant breast!

But you in lowly calm abide,
   Scarce heeded save by breeze or bee.
You know what splendor, pomp and pride
   Full oft your brilliant sisters see;
What sorrows, too, and bitter fears;
What mad farewells and hopeless tears!

How some are kept in old dear books,
   That once in bridal wreaths were worn;
How some are kissed, with tender looks,
   And later tossed aside with scorn;
How some their taintless petals lay
On icy foreheads, white as they!

So, while these truths you vaguely guess,
    Abloom in many a lonesome spot,
Shy roadside roses, may you bless
    The fate that rules your modest lot,
Like rustic maids that meekly stand
Below the ladies of their land!

A TUBEROSE.

CHASTE waxen shape, in whose clear chalice dwell
    Odors that tell
Of moans and tears and chambers gloomed with grief,
Wan sister of the tulip's laughing bloom,
    What primal doom
Fashioned the lifeless pallor of your leaf?

As winds down dreamy gardens came to sigh
    "The year must die,"
At some old immemorial twilight hour,
Did you, the incarnate terror and unrest
    Of summer's breast,
First bathe in chilling dews your ghostly flower?

Or did the moon, through some sweet night long-dead,
    Her splendor shed
On some rich tomb, while silence held its breath,
Till one pure sculptured blossom thrilled and grew
    Strangely to you,
Cold child of moonbeams, marble, and white death!

IVY.

Ill canst thou bide in alien lands like these,
    Whose home lies overseas,
Among manorial halls, parks wide and fair,
    Churches antique, and where
Long hedges flower in May and one can hark
To carollings from old England's lovely lark!

Ill canst thou bide where memories are so brief,
    Thou that hast bathed thy leaf
Deep in the shadowy past, and known strange things
    Of crumbled queens and kings;
Thou whose green kindred, in years half forgot,
Robed the gray battlements of proud Camelot!

Through all thy fibres' intricate expanse
    Hast thou breathed sweet romance;
Ladies that long are dust thou hast beheld
    Through dreamy days of eld;
Watched in broad castle-courts the merry light
Bathe gaudy banneret and resplendent knight!

And thou hast seen, on ancient lordly lawns,
    The timorous dappled fawns;
Heard pensive pages with their suave lutes play
    Some low Provençal lay;
Marked beauteous dames through arrased chambers
    glide,
With lazy graceful staghounds at their side!

And thou hast gazed on splendid cavalcades
    Of nobles, matrons, maids,
Winding from castle gates on breezy morns,
    With golden peals of horns,
In velvet and brocade, in plumes and silk,
With falcons, and with palfreys white as milk!

Through convent-casements thou hast peered, and there
    Viewed the meek nun at prayer;
Seen, through rich panes dyed purple, gold, and rose,
    Monks read old folios;
On abbey-walls heard wild laughs thrill thy vine
When the fat tonsured priests quaffed ruby wine!

O ivy, having lived in times like these,
    Here art thou ill at ease;
For thou art one with ages passed away,
    We are of yesterday!
Short retrospect, slight ancestry is ours,
But thy dark leaves clothe history's haughty towers!

HEMLOCKS.

(TERZA RIMA.)

I KNEW a forest, tranquil and august,
   Down whose green deeps my steps would often
     stray
When leisure met my life as dew meets dust!

Proud spacious chestnuts verged each winding way,
   And hickories in whose dry boughs winds were
     shrill,
And tremulous white-boled birches. Here, one day,

Strolling beside the scarce-held steed of will,
   I found a beautiful monastic grove
Of old primeval hemlocks, living still!

Round it the forest rustled, flashed, and throve,
   But here was only silence and much gloom,
As though some sorcerer in dead days had wove,

With solemn charms and muttered words of doom,
   A cogent spell that said to time "Depart!"
And locked it in the oblivion of a tomb!

Thick was its floor, where scant ferns dared to start,
   With tawny needles, and an old spring lay
Limpid as crystal in its dusky heart!

Vaguely enough can language ever say
   What sombre and fantastic dreams, for me,
Held shadowy revel in my thought that day!

How stern similitudes would dimly be
   Of painted braves that grouped about their king;
Or how, in crimson firelight, I would see

Some ghostly war-dance whose weak cries took wing
   Weirdly away beyond the grove's dark brink ;
Or how I seemed to watch, by that old spring,

The timid phantom deer steal up to drink !

THE ACORN.

I FIND you nestling in the balmy grass,
   Here where the knotty oak so stoutly stands,
While tremulous breezes with rich fragrance pass,
   Like ghosts with viewless flowers in viewless hands !

Frail germ of strength, I scan with eager heed,
   As from the summer sward I lift you up,
The tawny oval of your polished bead
   Bulging so smoothly from its rugged cup.

And now with heart where happy fancies meet,
   I stoop, and in the yielding meadow make
A grave wherefrom, with resurrection sweet,
   Some future sun shall win you to awake !

And while I plant you thus, I seem to plant
   Flutings of silver winds in ample boughs
That weave a gloom where sunbeams richly slant,
   Bees murmur, and the lazy cattle browse.

And now I seem to plant, below the green
   Of these fair ungrown boughs, at eve or morn,
The first delicious thrilling kiss between
   Two fond young lovers that are yet unborn !

FERNS.

IF trees are Nature's thoughts or dreams,
   And witness how her great heart yearns,
Then she has only shown, it seems,
   Her lightest fantasies in ferns.

Those low green boughs, what shapely grace,
   What slender lissome charm they wear,
Delicate, supple, frail as lace,
   And pliant to each passing air!

Though sweet to see when there or here,
   Along some common meadowed way,
They throng in feathery jungles, near
   Some stolid boulder's bulk of gray,

Yet ah! no light their spray so serves
   As when, where cloistering branches cross,
I meet its shadowy silvered curves
   On spaces of dark moonlit moss!

For here quick fancy finds a bower
   Where she can watch, in pictured wise,
An Oberon squeeze the fatal flower
   On poor Titania's drowsing eyes!

And nimble fay and pranksome elf
   Flash vaguely past at every turn,
Or, weird and wee, sits Puck himself,
   With legs akimbo, on a fern!

MOSS.

STRANGE tapestry, by Nature spun
  On viewless looms, aloof from sun,
   And spread through lonely nooks and grots
    Where shadows reign and leafy rest, —
  O moss, of all your dwelling-spots,
    In which one are you loveliest?

Is it when near grim roots that coil
Their snaky black through mellow soil?
   Or when you wrap, in woodland glooms,
    The great prone pine-trunks, rotted red?
   Or when you dim, on sombre tombs,
    The *requiescats* of the dead?

Or is it when your lot is cast
In some quaint garden of the past,
   On some gray crumbled basin's brim,
    Where mildewed Tritons conch-shells blow,
   While yonder, through the poplars prim,
    Looms up the turreted château?

Nay, loveliest are you when time weaves
Your emerald films on low dark eaves,
   Above where pink porch-roses peer
    And woodbines break in fragrant foam,
   And children laugh . . . and you can hear
    The beatings of the heart of Home!

LEAVES.

Οἵη περ φύλλων γενεὴ, τοιήδε καὶ ἀνδρῶν.

DEEP among forest-quietudes of green
   My steps have wandered, and about me now,
In soft complexities of shade and sheen,
   On many a lavish-clad midsummer bough,
The innumerous breezy leaves, above, around,
Move with melodious and aerial sound.

I pause to look, in meditative mood,
   Where all their murmurous myriads richly throng,
And think what touches of similitude,
   What dark or bright analogies belong
(As bonds that Nature's mystic shuttle weaves)
Between the lives of men and lives of leaves!

Some in the loftiest places burst their buds,
   And get the sun's gold kiss while they uncurl;
They front the stars and the proud moon that floods
   Pure domes of limpid heaven with airy pearl.
They see the damask of cool dawns; they gaze
On smiles that light the lips of dying days!

And some in lowlier places must abide,
   And gain but glimpses, perishably dear,
Of altering cloud and meadow glimmering wide,
   And the large lovely world beyond their sphere!
And some have rare dews thrill each thirsty stem,
Or rarelier yet, a bird's wing brushes them!

And some amid their perfect emerald prime
   Are torn from nurturing boughs at storm's caprice,
And some turn old and sere before their time,
   And flutter down as if in glad release.
And all to Autumn's bleak dismantling blast,
Even all, inevitably yield at last!

But when I mark how some that once were fair,
   From edge to edge in flawless gloss arrayed,
Must feel the worm's fang gnaw them through, like care,
   I seem to have dimly guessed why God has made
So many tremulous leaves, for their frail parts,
Wear, as they throb, the shapes of human hearts!

CLOVER.

WILD rustic cousins of the dainty rose,
   Whose fragrant banquets lure the greedy bees,
Haytime's pink prophecies while young June goes,
   How brightly spread your many-blossoming seas,
   Rippled whichever way the warm winds please!

Laughterful children feel your tufts of bloom
   Brush their soft limbs, alert with merry leaps.
The iridescent humming-bird's low boom
   With mellow music thrills your balmy deeps,
   Where dew that was born yesterday still sleeps!

Here, too, the massive lazy cow, star-eyed,
   Thrusts down her dark moist nose, and all day long,
By your delicious feast unsatisfied,
   Crops with rough florid tongue your honeyed throng,
   Lashing off flies with her tail's restless thong.

Or sometimes from your cool bournes, where it hid,
  A butterfly soars fluttering, breeze-assailed,
Gay as those flowery gondolas that slid
  Through sculptured Venice in old days, and trailed
  Brocades and velvets where they softly sailed!

O clover, tended by the shining showers
  Until your lavish color gladlier beams,
Or, through the yellow calms of morning hours,
  Dappled with interchange of glooms and gleams,
  Like vague recurrences of differing dreams,

Does Nature act in you her frankest part,
  And are you thoughts that she would simply say,
Speaking them right from her full-throbbing heart?
  Or were you made some more mysterious way,
  From damask blushes of young morns in May?

GRAPES.

AMID the arbor's amber-tarnished vine,
    Faint-fluttering to the South-wind's languid sigh,
  Under this drowsy haze of mellow sky,
The great grapes droop their dusty globes of wine!

And even amid these bland luxurious hours,
  They seem like exiles reft of cherished rights,
  Here in our treacherous North, whose Autumn nights
Drop chilly dews upon the dying flowers!

Ripe clusters, while our woods in ruin flame,
    Do yearnings through your rich blood vaguely thrill
    For glimmering vineyard, olive-mantled hill,
And Italy, which is summer's softer name?

Or do you dream of some old ducal board,
    Blazing with Venice glass and costliest plate,
    Where princely banqueters caroused in state,
And through the frescoed hall the long feast roared?

Or how brocaded dame and plumed grandee
    Saw your imperial-colored fruit heaped up
    On radiant salver or in chiselled cup,
Where some proud marble gallery faced the sea!

Or yet do your strange yearnings, loath to cease,
    Go wandering on till dearer visions rise
    Of the pale temples and the limpid skies,
The storied shores and haunted groves of Greece?

Greece, where the god was yours of such renown, —
    That sleek-limbed revelling boy, supremely fair,
    Who, with the ambrosial gold of his wild hair,
Would wreathe your purple opulence for a crown!

A TOAD.

BLUE dusk, that brings the dewy hours,
    Brings thee, of graceless form in sooth,
Dark stumbler at the roots of flowers,
    Flaccid, inert, uncouth.

Right ill can human wonder guess
    Thy meaning or thy mission here,
Gray lump of mottled clamminess,
    With that preposterous leer!

But when I meet thy dull bulk where
    Luxurious roses bend and burn,
Or some slim lily lifts to air
    Its frail and fragrant urn,

Of these, among the garden-ways,
    So grim a watcher dost thou seem,
That I, with meditative gaze,
    Look down on thee and dream

Of thick-lipped slaves, with ebon skin,
    That squat in hideous dumb repose,
And guard the drowsy ladies in
    Their still seraglios!

WEEDS.

I LEAN across the sagging gate;
   In rough neglect the garden lies,
Disfeatured and disconsolate
   Below these halcyon skies.

O'er pleasant ways once trimly kept,
   And blossoming fair at either verge,
Weeds in rank opulence have swept
   Their green annulling surge!

Order's pure wisdom they have crushed,
   With reckless feet, in rude disdain.
Like some gross rabble they have rushed
   On beauty's bright domain!

But over them, as though in soft
   Memory of bloom that no more blows,
A rose-bush rears one bough aloft,
   Starred with one stainless rose!

Above these weeds whose ruffian power
   So coarsely envies what is fair,
She bends her lightsome dainty flower
   With such patrician air,

That while I watch this chaste young rose,
   Some pale scared queen she seems to be,
Across whose palace-courtyard flows
   The dark mob, like a sea!

A BAT.

HAPHAZARD hybrid that one sees,
    Half bird, half reptile, fluttering through
Those sultry twilights when the trees
    Loom breezeless on the dreamy blue ;
Strange blundering mongrel of the air,
At random war with here and there,
    Now wheeling wild and swooping now ;
In what mad mood did Nature please
Her sweet rich harmonies to scare
    With such dark dissonance as thou ?
    Shape that unseemliest traits endow,
Grotesque, chimeric, cold, impure,
With Satan's wings in miniature !

Nay, is it that thou lingerest here
    As the last-left weak heir of what
Survives from many a wrecking year
    In shadowy fable, trusted not ?
Does altered time in thee behold
One waif from horrors manifold,
    Ghoul, griffon, dragon, ouph, gnome, sprite,
That living shook the world with fear,
And dying when the earth was old,
    In mockery of their crumbled might
    Foredoomed thy tortuous dismal flight
Where once by terror and dismay
Thine awful ancestry held sway ?

BOX.

THE path from porch to gate I rim,
In rounded clusters rising trim.
With changeless mien, I lift serene
My small bright leaves of dusky green.

I droop not under blinding heat,
Nor shrink from savage cold and sleet;
When o'er me flow pale shrouds of snow,
My patient verdure thrives below.

I cannot lure the dainty bee;
No breeze of summer sighs for me;
In sombre mood I drowse and brood,
With memory-haunted quietude.

For though I guard a sturdy strength,
My life has known unwonted length;
Fair days or dark I mutely mark,
The garden's tranquil patriarch.

That white-haired lady, frail of form,
Who seeks the porch when suns are warm,
Has near me smiled, a blithesome child,
With tangled ringlets tossing wild.

As years went on, with air sedate
She met her love at yonder gate.
I saw him bring, one night in Spring,
The precious gold betrothal-ring!

To church along this path she went,
A twelvemonth later, well-content.
With peerless charm, in sweet alarm,
She leaned upon her father's arm.

Again to church, when years had fled,
In widow's dress, with bended head,
I saw her guide at either side
Her black-robed children, pensive-eyed.

These children now are dames and men,
But I to-day am young as then;
And yet each rose that near me blows
Laughs lightly at my prim repose.

Ah, giddy flowers that briefly live,
Your thoughtless whispers I forgive,
Since calmly I, as years go by,
In damask thousands watch you die!

DEW.

SOFT tears that Nature keeps to show,
   In human way, her joys and pains,
Now shed when summer splendors glow,
   Or now when gaudy Autumn reigns!

Chaste pearls, whose lustres love to hide
   In deeps of grassy seas for hours!
Dear secrets that the skies confide
   To the warm bosoms of the flowers!

Kind almoners, that hold as peers
   Proud garden or wild woodland maze!
Beautiful nightly souvenirs
   Of all the perished elves and fays!

Cool benedictions of the dawn!
   Eve's lowlier starlight, vague and shy!
Profoundly is my spirit drawn
   By your sweet spells to question why

So many hearts, as flowers might do,
   Dry lips in thirsting pain must tend,
And though they dumbly plead for dew,
   Must die without it in the end!

FIREFLIES.

I SAW, one sultry night, above a swamp,
 The darkness throbbing with their golden pomp!

And long my dazzled sight did they entrance
With the weird chaos of their dizzy dance!

Quicker than yellow leaves, when gales despoil,
Quivered the brilliance of their mute turmoil,

Within whose light was intricately blent
Perpetual rise, perpetual descent,

As though their scintillant flickerings had met
In the vague meshes of some airy net!

And now mysteriously I seemed to guess,
While watching their tumultuous loveliness,

What fervor of deep passion strangely thrives
In the warm richness of these tropic lives,

Whose wings can never tremble but they show
These hearts of living fire that beat below!

FOUR DAYS.

I.

NOW are the moments, brief and rare,
   When Nature warms with subtle bliss,
Like some chaste maiden, shy of air,
   Who gives her lover the first kiss !

The willows o'er the flashing brook
   Bow lissome, with fresh-mantled stem,
Like graceful ladies when they look
   To find their mirrors praising them !

The orchard-aisles, that blooms array
   In odorous mimicry of snow,
Are thrilled through every happy spray
   With song's mellifluous overflow !

And all the world, with greens that shine,
   With breaking buds and wings that flit,
Seems one expectancy divine
   Of something God has promised it !

II.

White fleeces load the deep-blue day;
   Long fitful breezes haunt its calm,
Like sweet thieves flying in dismay
   From far Hesperides of balm !

The giddy bee, with murmur keen,
    Reels o'er the garden's brightest reach;
The sly wasp hovers, black and lean,
    Above the pink luxurious peach.

No gaudy currants drape their bough,
    Erewhile with luscious crimson twined,
But here large velvet leaves o'erbrow
    The yellowing melon's figured rind.

And here a pumpkin's lazy gold
    Has slowly greatened more and more,
Till now its heart might almost hold
    Cinderella's fairy coach-and-four!

III.

This broad wood, in whose blighted ways,
    Along damp sward, I stroll and muse,
To winds of rapid vigor sways,
    One halcyon tanglement of hues!

Yet I can never walk an hour
    Where all these hollow grandeurs gleam,
And watch the land's great passion-flower
    Of beauteous anguish, but I dream

How lofty lives have played their parts,
    Feigning in splendor false content;
How gorgeous robes o'er broken hearts
    Have made despair magnificent!

Or how, at Borgia feasts, long since,
   Where lavish pomp spread costly signs,
Death, the dark slave of priest and prince,
   Waited in those voluptuous wines!

IV.

Last night the air was dense with sleet,
   And now I mark, with smothered sigh,
The pale blank meadows lapse to meet
   A leaden monotone of sky!

O colorless and glacial gloom!
   O earthly torpor, bleak and stern!
Have the blithe charms of bird or bloom
   Gone forth to nevermore return? . . .

What dreary mood has fancy found?
   Steal up, dear love, and break the spell! . . .
Her lightsome footsteps faintly sound . . .
   You come, dear love, and all is well!

For now your blushes look to me
   Like June's first roses, freshly gay,
And in your deep eyes one can see
   The violets tarrying till May!

II.

VOICES AND VISIONS.

THE HOUSE ON THE HILL.

I HAVE not blamed him; I shall not blame;
   It is best for him, though bitter for me,
Whose poor heart holds the past the same
   As a box of gems with a missing key!

For Philip was born to shine, you know;
   I can never help, through my darkest pain,
Being glad he should win the world, and so
   Gain early all that he ought to gain.

It used to seem, in the old dead days,
   A marvel that he should find one trace
Of charm in a girl with my plain ways,
   And timidly unimportant face.

His frame for a sculptor might have served;
   His hair, over deep-blue eyes and clear,
Grew high on the temples ere it curved
   In rich crisp gold round the shapely ear.

And I think there are few things like his smile,
   Or his laugh's full mellow sweetness, too;
And then, in his own wild self-taught style,
   He was clever beyond all men I knew.

And often, indeed, throughout each year,
   He would read his poems to me alone,
While I tried to make my whole soul hear,
   With his strong man's hand in both my own!

And some I would find most grave and grand,
   And some to my eyes the hot tears sent,
And some I would ache to understand,
   But not know a word of what they meant!

For Phil was to me like a land that keeps
   High cliffs it dazzles the eye to trace,
Though I cared not much for the lofty steeps,
   While violets blossomed about their base!

But 'twas pleasure to know him well above
   The throng of his fellows, I avow;
For woman's pride is to woman's love
   More closely wedded than leaf to bough!

And so when that summer came at last
   Which made the old house on the hill look gay,
Its silence being a thing of the past
   And its shadowy chambers blest with day,

Why, what seemed likelier to my thought,
   If I stayed to think, than that my dear Phil,
For the graceful gifts his presence brought,
   Should be welcomed at the house on the hill?

And his welcomers chose, for their fine part,
   So to scatter favors about his feet,
That I grew at length to be sure in heart
   Of just the nights when we would not meet.

He would tell me of their soft household ease
  And their manners, touched with a fine repose,
And of all they had borne across the seas
  From lands of sun and from lands of snows.

And deep was my pleasure to hear him speak
  Of how warmly all would greet him there,
From the proud old dame with the faded cheek
  To the rosy pet with the reckless hair.

But as summer died amid waning wealth,
  A something in Phil seemed also dead,
And now and then I would weep by stealth,
  For my soul grew dark with a nameless dread!

He was shadowed with gloomy change and cold,
  That made, while it put the past to scorn,
His kiss of now by his kiss of old
  Seem a wilted rose by a rose just born!

And the change grew worse; but I played a part,
  And gave no sign, in my stubborn pride,
While doubt knocked loud at the door of my heart,
  Like a guest that will not be denied!

But at last it was all made plain as day! . . .
  Though she who told it me meant the best,
How the gold in the sunny air turned gray,
  How the youth died out from my aching breast!

'Twas my old friend, Ellen, who spoke and showed
  The truth, one morn, with her true bold tongue,
As we met on the same elm-bordered road
  Which had led to school when we both were young.

"You have keen eyes, Kate, but you will not see,
　Quick ears, yet you strangely fail to hear!
Your Philip is false as a man may be,
　For all that you hold his love so dear!

" I will speak the truth, though its shock should kill;
　God help me, too, if I go amiss!
They greet him well at the house on the hill,
　Yet ah! . . . there is something more than this!

"There is one who rules him with fatal sway,
　Who turns his heart from its loyal place;
A girl with brown hair waving away
　From a clear-cut pale patrician face.

" The babbled lies of the gossip-cliques
　I meet with loathing, I stand above;
But, Kate, what it all has meant for weeks
　Heaven only knows if it be not love!

" They were strolling slowly, this very morn,
　On the lonely roadside where I came,
And before my kindling look of scorn
　He dropt his eyes with a flush of shame.

" Oh, Kate, he is faithless through and through;
　'Tis a base mean game that he plays by stealth;
For he turns like a churl away from you,
　To fawn with a smile at the feet of wealth!"

So Ellen spoke; and an eager kiss
　Came warm from her lips against my own;
But nothing is quite clear, after this,
　Till I stood in my little room alone.

I stood, and all in a moment brief,
  With a cry my lips could not control,
Sank quivering to the floor, and grief
  Wrung up the sobs from my secret soul!
. . . .
That night he came, and I met him just
  At the old porch-steps, worn wry with years.
The air was keen, but I would not trust
  A light on the traces of my tears.

As he took my tremulous hand, I spoke:
  "Let us walk for a little while" . . . But here
My voice into wretched tremor broke,
  Though I tried so hard to make it clear.

Then he knew that I knew it all at last,
  And with bowed head murmured, "As you please;"
And down through the garden-paths we past,
  In silence under the sighing trees.

I remember the night so well, so well! . . .
  The foliage moved with a sad unrest,
And a large deep-crimson crescent fell
  Through the pale-blue air of the starry West.

And heavy and cold as a hand of doom
  Had the Autumn dewfall come to set
Its chill on the chaste tuberose's bloom
  And the low close copse of the mignonette.

And haunting the dark, and seeming thus
  To hold it in sad mysterious thrall,
The voice of the katydid came to us
  In weird, monotonous, plaintive call.

He walked with his head bent, still as stone,
    And now, since I saw he would not speak,
I spoke myself, with a quivering tone
    And a great hot tear on either cheek.

"Philip," I said, "'twas a bitter wrong
    To have done your soul that for such as I
You should trifle with sacred truth so long,
    And soil white honor, and live a lie!

"Had you frankly warned me when love first died,
    While you turned in spirit from her to me,
Can you doubt what my lips had then replied,
    Though it dealt me death to set you free?

"Yet I must not chide you for changing, Phil;
    I know my worth; can I fail to know
How all along we were mated ill,
    You that are lofty, I that am low?

"I shall prize my past, though its light will seem
    As the flash of a bird's wing seen afar,
For old love remembers young love's dream
    As twilight remembers the morning-star!

"All thought should be dear of its lost repose
    To the aching frame of the storm-worn ship,
And dear all thought to the thirsty rose
    Of the dew once glittering at its lip!

"And to me shall be dear all thought of yore,
    As its green to the leaf now gray with frost,
As the crown to the brow it girds no more,
    As the sea to the pearl it loved and lost!"

Now I paused, and now for a little space
   I watched him tremble and try to speak,
And saw, as the moonlight struck his face,
   The white we see on a dead man's cheek.

"Ah, Kate," he murmured, "you cannot guess
   How this heart of mine, as it hears you, feels
To its guilty centre the shock and stress
   Of the blow your noble pardon deals!

"Having so wronged you, I could but count
   That a righteous wrath in your look would shine,
Nor ever dream that your soul would mount
   To grasp at a vengeance so divine!

"But, Kate, if shame can the past repair,
   From this life you were blameless to despise
Take all that your just contempt can spare,
   And let it serve you until it dies!

"And perhaps your love, with its deeps untold,
   Shall have gained the power, I dream not how,
To see the man you knew me of old
   In the worthless traitor you know me now!"

As he ceased, I thrilled with a yearning thrill,
   But I said, in words that were cold and slow,
"Answer me what I shall ask of you, Phil;
   On your honor answer it, — yes or no!

"Which of us two has your heart this night?
   Speak truth: is it here or yonder, Phil?
Here, where we stand in the mellow light,
   Or yonder, — at the house on the hill?"

I questioned thus, though I did not dare
  Look once on his white face, vague to see,
But with dropt eyes felt, as I waited there,
  That the world stood still till he answered me!

So, waiting near him, with bended head
  And with palm to palm held firm and tense,
I seemed, while the meagre moments fled,
  To be living a lifetime of suspense!

And now, with a stifled sob, I sent
  A prayer to the God who makes or mars,
That out from my longing bosom went,
  Like a bird let forth from its prison-bars!

I prayed that my new hope might not flit
  As a dream back to dreamland, past recall;
And I prayed . . . but alas! what profits it
  To remember now that I prayed at all?

My hand on a sudden he caught and pressed,
  While he said, in a whisper strange and rough:
"Yes, Kate, — God help me! — I love *her* best.
  You ask for truth: I have lied enough."

(So the prayer was vain! So the hope was fled!)
  Then I sighed, though he did not hear me sigh,
And I let him keep my hand as I said,
  "The truth is better. Good-night, — good-bye."...

It was dark by this, for the moon hung low;
  And I heard the katydid's wild clear cry,
As it rang from meadowy reaches, grow
  Like an echoing voice . . . *Good-night! good-bye!*

FIDELITAS.

Dost thou dream I forget thee, O star that hast fled
   From a heaven where its light lingers yet?
Since we parted with pangs, to thy soul hast thou said
   That my love would forego and forget?

Do not fear; it is love that, though prisoned apart
   From thine own for long ages, would be
As the shell flung ashore that yet hides in its heart
   All the sounds of the songs of the sea!

I shall live out my life, I shall draw daily breath,
   Shall endure, yet in such wounded wise
As the stag that goes wearily, smitten with death,
   To the pool that it drinks of and dies!

'Tis in vain that the years, though they labor, shall bring
   For my anguish Nepenthean wine.
As the sword to the scabbard, the plume to the wing,
   O my love, was thy life unto mine!

And with infinite sorrow my spirit has seen
   How a gulf never sounded nor crost,
In its blackness of darkness yawns awful between
   The words "I have loved" — "I have lost."

But as bells in the belfries and spires of the past,
    Shall my dreams of thee changelessly chime,
And the rock of my passion shall wear at the last
    Not a scar from the tempest of time!

When my heart to the bourne of no comfort may turn
    That can lighten its loss or repair,
Shall the star of its longing not lovelier burn
    In the deepening night of despair?

And for love to the cross of remembrance to cling
    Is not more in its effort with me
Than for leafage to mistily glimmer in Spring
    On the wreck of a storm-ruined tree!

I shall foster no fear that my soul may forget,
    While in reaches of innermost thought
The immutable marble of deathless regret
    To an image of thee has been wrought!

And if ever that image doth seem to uprise
    Through a gloom whose vague fitfulness dims,
'Tis from tears dropping down out of memory's eyes
    On the lamp that she watches and trims!

ADORATION.

I HAVE sought the intensest ways to best adore you,
   I have laid my soul's last treasure at your feet;
Yet I tremble as in thought I bend before you
   With abasement and abashment and defeat,
Knowing well that all the love I ever bore you
   Is requital weak of worth and incomplete!

As one might seize a lyre, across it sweeping
   His fleet precipitate hand that has no care,
Imperiously upon the strained strings heaping
   A mightier melody than these can bear,
So love has taken my life within his keeping
   And smitten it with great strokes that scorn to spare!

I am less than that which thrills me and entrances,
   As a wounded bird is less than they that fly;
As the suppliant surge that arches and advances
   Than the resolute rock-mass where it comes to die;
As a violet's color than the bland expanses,
   The unshadowed calms of overcurving sky!

Desiring from my soul to have given you greatly
   Of my thanks for your great love-gift given to me,
I am slight as some poor rivulet flowing straitly
   Near all the abundant splendors of the sea,
And my worship is as nothingness by the stately
   Magnificence of what it fain would be!

Over my soul, in hours of meditation,
    Murmurs a voice with monotones that tire :
God meant not that from this deep adoration
    This vehement joy should fill me and should fire,
Looking on life in passionate elation
    From heights that so transcendently aspire !

Full soon, I know it, while they shall strain to free not,
    From these idolatrous arms you shall be torn ;
You are fated from my days to pass and be not,
    Like all of rare and fair they have ever worn ;
I am doomed, although the stealthy doom I see not ;
    I feast, albeit I die to-morrow morn !

You or your love, it is fated, soon shall falter,
    And vanish away, since here no sweet thing dwells ;
No voice among blithe birds that take for psalter
    The world at Springtide, carolling what it tells ;
No light, no flower, no moon that fails to alter,
    No song, no mellow minglement of bells !

Yet though you vanish, memory shall cling dust-like
    To hours when your first kiss first met my mouth !
Though on loved lands the annulling snow lie crust-like,
    Can we forget the old winds that blew from South ?
Forget the old green of lands where lingers rust-like
    The dull disfeaturing leprosy of drouth ?

And I, in reverent and memorial manner,
    Shall dream of you divinely and be stirred,
As sad Arcadia dreams of how Diana
    Made silvery limbs and laughter seen or heard ;

As some rude crag-tower that wild grasses banner,
   Dreams of how lit there some great strange white
      bird!

Yet let me at least love fortune while she blesses,
   Nor vainly cavil at bliss because it flies;
Let me not dim the sun with doubts and guesses,
   But pluck the flower-like day before it dies;
Catch the fleet hour by back-flung robe or tresses,
   And plunge a long strong look in her sweet eyes!

But ah! the vanity of desire, when kneeling
   We yearn for utterance that no god will teach!
When, at the finite bounded heart's appealing,
   An infinite boundless love evades its reach!
When the waves of deep ungovernable feeling
   Dash powerless on the baffling gates of speech!

My fervidest language hath an utter lightness,
   My deeds devoutest are as deeds undone,
Do I mark your marble arm that slopes to slightness,
   Or see the clear smile at your lips begun!
That opulent smile beneath whose lavish brightness
   You are like a lily overbrimmed with sun!

Who am I for whom the hand of hope is sending
   Her freshest olive-spray, her dearest dove?
Who am I that thus, though made for mortal ending,
   I sit Alcides-like with gods above?
Who am I that dare, however lowly-bending,
   Be laurelled with the chaplet of your love?

How am I blest that have not met with scorning,
   Yet walk where worthier feet might well have trod,
Being thrilled as earth, at April's earliest warning,
   Through amplitudes of winter-withered sod,
Or shadowy meadows when the feet of morning
   Are beautiful upon the hills of God !

The illimited love I bear you ever urges
   My ardent soul through deeps of distance new,
While far aloof, where mind in spirit merges,
   Fresh deeps of distance ever rise to view,
Like those dim lines that seem, o'er leagues of surges,
   Bastions of mist below the vaulted blue !

O for a hand its ruinous blows to dash on
   The expansive spirit's narrowing chains and bars !
O for a voice that lordlier phrase might fashion
   Than this cold human phrase which frets and mars !
O for a heart with room for all its passion,
   As hollow heaven has room for all her stars !

IF TRULY.

IF truly thou art still the same,
    Deep-eyed, soft-speaking as of old ;
  If nothing strange or sad or cold,
  Nothing that hints of tears untold,
Nothing that one might name or might not name,
Meeting thee after these flown years, be seen,
To mar the accustomed sweetness of thy mien,
    Then surely 'tis not mine to chide
    Harsh fate, being satisfied !

If truly thou art happy, this
    Alone suffices, love, to me !
    If all that I might ever be
    That other now has grown ; if he
Awakes the pure deep thrills of utter bliss
I had believed one only could awake ;
If he has found the secret that can make
    Thy days to music glide, —
    Enough . . . I am satisfied !

DARKNESS.

I HAD a dream of a wild-lit place
    Where three dark spirits met face to face.

One said: "I am darkest; I had birth
In the central blackness of mid-earth."

With a sneer one said, below his breath:
"I am still more dark, for I am Death."

But the third, with voice that bleaker pealed
Than freezing wind on a houseless field,

Cried, where he stood from the rest apart,
"I am that darkness which fills man's heart

"When it aches and yearns and burns for one
It has loved as the meadow loves the sun!"

Now I gazed on him from earth's mid-reach,
And now on the spirit of death; and each,

Though dark with a darkness to affright,
Beside that third was a shape of light!

HIS CHILD.

(A Woman speaks.)

AH, how may finite language tell
The boundless pain of that farewell!

At last I pleaded, speaking low
Between great sobs, " In mercy go!"

He did not speak, but, stooping now,
Laid one long kiss against my brow!

Then, when a little space had flown,
I stood for evermore alone!

Wounded in spirit. dazed, aghast,
I had no future but my past!

Yet time, that heeds not joys or fears,
Inexorably shaped its years.

But years like weak waves broke above
The changeless granite of my love!

The world, that thought this love was dead,
Praised the sweet woman he had wed!

I heard its praise; I gave no sign;
Yet ah! what agony was mine!

Within my life there came a day
When past his home my journey lay.

The lawns flowed wide in grassy seas,
The house was hid with stately trees;

And in the gateway, sweetly fair,
A young child stood, with shining hair.

I paused a moment by the gate ....
I trembled with a deadly hate!

In this frail child I seemed to see
My own despair confronting me!

Yet while I watched the child, there stole
A lovely change across my soul!

He gazed upon me in surprise;
He thrilled me with his father's eyes!

Then, as I gently drew more near,
He gently smiled, and had no fear.

And now, all feeling unrepressed,
I knelt and caught him to my breast!

And blinded with hot tears, I now
Laid one long kiss against his brow!

SELF-DECEPTION.

SCORNING my stubborn love, that can but see
   Your stubborn scorn, that alters by no breath,
I shut my teeth and cry, " It shall not be !
   I will not drag this shackle down to death ! "

And so I make a wall of absence rise
   And grow between us, till at length I seem
To view my stormy past with stern surprise,
   Bathed in the drowsy mezzo-tint of dream !

And after lapsing time there comes a day
   When, proud of this calm strength that fills my breast,
I hear the very voice of courage say,
   " Be bold, and put thy vaunted power to test ! "

We meet : through all my blood one thrill is sent,
   And suddenly, in a moment, where I stand,
The illusive faith on which my life has leant
   Cracks like a rotten staff beneath my hand !

And even as one that has been drugged with wine
   And left by revellers on some couch to loll,
Love, with pale moaning lips, with eyes that shine,
   Wakes in the shadowy chamber of my soul !

CHIAROSCURO.

THE garden, with its throngs of drowsy roses,
  Below the suave midsummer night reposes,
And here kneel I, whom fate supremely blesses,
In the dim room, whose lamplit dusk discloses
Your two dark stars of eyes, your rippled tresses,
Whose fragrant folds the fragrant breeze caresses!

White flower of womanhood, ah! how completely,
How strongly, with invisible bonds, yet sweetly,
You bind, as my allegiant love confesses,
You bind, you bend, immutably and meetly,
This soul of mine, that all its pride represses,
A willing falcon in love's golden jesses!

To me such hours as these I breathe are holy!
I kneel, I tremble, I am very lowly
While this dear consecrated night progresses,
And faint winds through the lattice-vines float slowly
From all high starriest reaches and recesses,
Night's heavenly but unseen embassadresses!

A BIRD OF PASSAGE.

AS the day's last light is dying,
    As the night's first breeze is sighing,
I send you, Love, like a messenger-dove, my thought
    through the distance flying!
    Let it perch on your sill; or, better,
    Let it feel your soft hand's fetter,
While you search and bring from under its wing, love,
    hidden away like a letter!

A LEAVE-TAKING.

THEY stand and see the sunset make
  A whorl of scarlet in the West,
    And white before them
See meadowfuls of daisies break
  Wavelike at every wind's behest
    That wanders o'er them.

He is a man of easeful air,
  Of genial youth, of happy grace
    In form and vesture:
She is a girl with glimmering hair,
  Deep eyes, and mobile oval face,
    And gentle gesture.

He plucks a grass-blade from the ground,
  And idly tears it as he speaks,
    And laughs, and lingers;
She swings a wild-rose she has found,
  Chaste-colored like her own fair cheeks,
    Between two fingers.

He takes his leave, with proffered palm,
  With words half serious, half in jest, —
    A light leave-taking.
She answers, careless, courteous, calm:
  (He does not dream that in her breast
    The heart is breaking!)

VESTA.

WHEN skies are starless yet when day is done,
   When odors of the freshened sward are sweeter,
When light is dreamy round the sunken sun,
   At limit of the grassy lane I meet her.

She steals a gracious hand across the gate;
   My own its timid touch an instant flatters;
Below the glooming leaves we linger late,
   And gossip of a thousand airy matters.

I gladden that the hay is stored with luck;
   I smile to hear the pumpkin-bed is turning;
I mourn the lameness of her speckled duck;
   I marvel at the triumphs of her churning.

From cow to cabbage and from horse to hen,
   I treat bucolics with my rustic charmer,
At heart the most unpastoral of men,
   Converted by this dainty little farmer.

And yet if one soft syllable I chance,
   As late below the glooming leaves we linger,
The pretty veto sparkles in her glance,
   And cautions in her brown up-lifted finger.

O happy trysts at blossom-time of stars!
   O moments when the glad blood thrills and quickens!
O all-inviolable gateway-bars!
   O Vesta of the milking-pails and chickens!

ONE NIGHT IN SEVILLE.

HIGH and yet higher the slow moon arose,
    Mounting in majesty full-orbed and fair,
Till loftily o'er Seville's pale repose
    The great Giralda towered in opal air!

With vagueness all the rich-hued roofs were blent;
    Scarce might you tell their lilac from their green;
On languorous breezes came the pungent scent
    Of odorous alamedas, faintly seen.

Out from the crowded plaza floated light
    A peal of mirth or dulcet trill of song,
And brightening softly to the brightening night,
    The shadowy Guadalquivir lapsed along!

The flash of teeth, the gleam of combs, the dark
    Mantillas, the quaint gear of old and young,
The rustle of fans, the cigarillo's spark,
    The mellow-syllabled Sevillian tongue!

All these in pleasured memory still are fresh,
    But ah! that faultless face which came and fled,
Beaming amid its drapery's dusky mesh
    From the dim balcony above my head!

That face which for a fleet while glimmering through
    The abundant jasmines, thrilled me with surprise!
A drowsy smile, two dimpling cheeks and two
    Fathomless velvet Andalusian eyes!

A face so marvellous that one rash star,
  To see of beauty this rare flower and crown,
Leaned out in heaven its golden head too far,
  And dropt, a meteor, over Seville town!

BARCAROLLE.

THE lake lies with the sheen on it
  Of day's last look serene on it,
And round its rim in the gloaming dim the shades of
    the low hills lean on it!
  No slightest sound the charmful quiet mars;
  The hollow heaven is yearning for its stars!

  With strange half-proud humility,
  With sumptuous tranquillity,
Thou art lounging, Sweet, at my flattered feet, in stat-
    uesque immobility,
  Against thy bosom's chaste superb repose
  One heavy blood-red velvet-petalled rose!

  Thine affluent hair, so billowlike,
  The bends of thy form, so willowlike,
Thy face so clear from the red cachemire folded under
    its pale cheek pillowlike;
  The unrippled lake, the gloom, the calm . . .
    all dower
  Memory with one imperishable hour!

While we drift now to leeward, Love,
I can feel my life turn theeward, Love,
As a blossom will see some great gold bee and bow all
 its beauty beeward, Love!
From thine eyes' night my perfect day is made!
I seek them, as the ivy seeks the shade!

Look how the pines loom towerwise,
Skirting the lake-edge bowerwise!
The stars wait still ere they flock to fill the heavenly
 meadows flowerwise!
But Hesper in the darkening West burns now,
Like some grand diamond on some swart queen's
 brow!

Ah, Love, with the rich day failing so,
With the summer sunset paling so,
I would always rest on the lustrous breast of the lake,
 forever sailing so,
And feel, at languorous rapture's utmost goal,
Peace lightly sweep the lute-strings of my soul!

Heedless if skies be thunderful,
Heedless if time be plunderful,
And only sure of the splendor pure in those fathomless
 eyes and wonderful,
My soul would soar beyond all time, as soars
The upleaping lark through dawn's white corri-
 dors!

CRADLE-SONG.

I.

WINDILY over the rocking sea and windily over
      the damp dim grasses.
   Hark how the lowering Autumn night sweeps down
      on the lonely world !
Sombrely from the silver sunset hurry the storm's
      cloud-masses ;
   Out on the black and perilous water, cavernous
      waves are curled !

   Go to sleep, darling : go to sleep, dear one :
      Heed not the tempest gathering o'er thee !
   Slumber well, though the night be a drear one,
      Watched, my babe, by the mother that bore thee !

II.

While in my desolate home I listen, compassed about
      with the deepening darkness,
   Memory brings me her woful phantom, haunting the
      chilly gloom.
Oh, but the skies were bleak, that dawn, when he lay
      in his fearful starkness,
   Flung by the stern defiant waves where the dumb
      gray boulders loom !

Go to sleep, darling ; go to sleep, dear one ;
Heed not the tempest gathering o'er thee !
Slumber well, though the night be a drear one,
Wild and drear to the mother that bore thee !

III.

Cruelly in his dying face was flung the scorn of your moanful surges,
　Haughty sea, that hast left to love me this poor babe alone !
Hear not the voices, O my Sweet, that are singing thy father's dirges !
　Find in the Paradise of thy dreams the angel that he is grown !

Go to sleep, darling ; go to sleep, dear one ;
Heed not the tempest gathering o'er thee.
Slumber well, though the night be a drear one,
Watched by God and the mother that bore thee !

ONE MAY NIGHT.

HOW blandly, Love, this air of evening slips
  In from the drowsy violets to your lips !
If I were some great painter, I would draw
Your splendor of cool shoulder without flaw ;
Your arms, like those the boy of Ida kist,
Each wavering to its wonder of white wrist ;
Your throat, o'er which your face's full flower glows,
A stem so stately to so grand a rose !
And while I wrought them, burn beneath a spell
That smiles and tears must interblend to tell !

But lift toward me that fragrant mouth : for why
Should a mere breeze be deeplier blest than I ?
Were not these heavy blue-black tresses made
The swart broad molding of your brows to shade,
As shaded once the locks of Egypt's queen
Brows where the jewelled sparrow blazed in sheen ?
For hearts to have, life holds no lovelier thing
Within her hands than love and youth and Spring ;
Yet gazing on your fresh cheek one should say,
Though Winter were at wildest —" It is May ! "

FORGETFULNESS.

AFTER the long monotonous months, and after
  Vague yearnings as of suppliant viewless hands,
The first full note of Spring's aerial laughter
  Was wavering o'er the winter-wearied lands.

All earth seemed rich in sweet emancipations
  For all that frost so bitterly enslaves,
And, tended as with unseen ministrations,
  The sward grew fresh about the village graves!

And while I lingered in the halcyon weather
  To watch the tranquil churchyard, brightening fast,
My friend and his young wife rode by together, —
  Rode by and gave me greeting as they past.

They seemed like lovers with the choicest graces
  Of favoring fortune at their love's control,
Yet, as I looked upon their fleeting faces,
  A chill of recollection touched my soul!

For only two short Springtides had been numbered
  Since here among these graves, it then befell,
A grave was wrought beneath whose slab now slumbered
  The woman whom my friend had loved so well!

A gloom across the brilliant day came stealing,
  Whose darkness held the spirit from escape.
I saw my friend within a dim room, kneeling
  In haggard anguish by a sheeted shape!

FORGETFULNESS.

A chilly breeze across the chamber fluttered,
   Making the timorous night-light wax and wane,
And wearily on the roof above were uttered
   The low persistent requiems of the rain!

I thought of his great sobs and mien heart broken,
   His moans of agony and his wild-eyed stare,
And how the assuaging words I would have spoken
   Died at my lips before his deep despair!

" And now," I thought, " what worth his protestations,
   His tears, his pangs and all the grief he gave,
When, tended as with unseen ministrations,
   The sward grows green round her forgotten grave?"

And yet the brilliant day, divine for tidings
   Of cheerful change in all its ample glow,
Touched me with tender yet with potent chidings,
   And softly murmured, " It is better so!"

" Ah, yes," I mused, " immeasurably better
   To win suave healing from the fluctuant years;
To snap the bond of grief's tyrannic fetter:
   To let new hopes arch rainbows among tears!"

And now it seemed that Spring, the elate new-comer,
   Laughed out: " Oh, better all regret were brief!
Better the opulence of another summer
   Than last year's empty nest and shrivelled leaf!"

" Yes, better!" I made mute reiterations,
   But turned sad eyes to one green turfy wave,
Where, tended as with unseen ministrations,
   The sward grew fresh round that forgotten grave!

Oh, sweet it is when hope's white arms are wreathing
   Necks bowéd with sorrow, as they droop forlorn !
But ah ! the imperishable pathos breathing
   About those dead whom we no longer mourn !

SOUVENIR.

DARK hickory-boughs against blue shining sea ;
   Sharp-shapen fir-trees pluming sombre rocks ;
The cadence of wind-murmurs fresh and free ;
   The merry sunlight on brown girlish locks ;
The sounding of two tender voices low . . .
      And all so long ago !

A building of sweet castles in the air,
   Frail as the slim calm cloud o'er distant seas ;
Delicious idlesse ; carelessness of care ;
   Fragments of song ; unutterable ease !
Life's music at soft pianissimo . . . .
      And all so long ago !

A purple whorl of sunset in the West :
   A great gold star through a wide oriel seen ;
Two lilied hands upon a placid breast ;
   A mute pale face, ineffably serene !
A mourner kneeling in impassioned woe . . .
      And all so long ago !

THE MEETING.

I SAW in dreams a dim bleak heath,
   Where towered a gaunt pine by a rock,
And suddenly, from the earth beneath,
   That rent itself with an angry shock,
A shape sprang forth to that wild place,
Whose limbs by chains were trenched and marred,
And whose sardonic pain-worn face
   Was grimly scorched and scarred.

He waited by the spectral pine;
   Aloft he lifted haggard eyes;
A woman's form, of mien divine,
   Dropt earthward in seraphic wise.
Chaste as though bathed in breaking day,
   And radiant with all saintly charms,
She flew toward him till she lay
   Close-locked in his dark arms!

I heard a far vague voice that said:
   "On earth these twain had loved so well
That now their lives, when both are dead,
   Burst the great bounds of Heaven and Hell.
Alike o'er powers of gloom and light
   Prevailed their fervid prayers and tears;
They meet on this bleak heath one night
   In every thousand years!"

D'OUTRE MORT.

AND so 'tis over at last;
The passion and pain are past;
Death has him and holds him fast!

And now to the chamber dumb
Of his death-sleep white and numb,
Who of all earth should come

To look on him where he lies,
With her two cold stars of eyes,
And sigh the old common sighs, —

Who should stand by his bed,
In her sadness so well-bred,
With just the right poise of head,

But she, this woman he bore,
Through life till his life was o'er,
Such infinite yearning for?

And now she stands by his bed,
Forgetting to try and shed
One tear, as she sees him dead.

And when those about her fare
From the room, with solemn air,
She follows, leaving him there.

But just as she nears the door,
There drops on the shadowed floor
A sweet rich rose that she wore.

It drops, and she does not know,
And so lets it lie, and so
Goes out as the others go.

. . . .

Now they that next draw near
This man, in his sleep austere,
Find, shrinking away with fear,

That a rose, once bright and bland,
Is crushed in his frigid hand . . .
And they cannot understand ! . . .

FROM SHADOWLAND.

WHEN I lay weak and white on my death-bed,
      I smiled and said:
"Oh, soul, thine hour is near! Be comforted!"

And sweet at last it was to break away
      From bonds of clay,
And leap, a bodiless rapture, into day!

"For now," I thought, "this woman whose mute scorn
      My life has borne,
Crowned with it even as with a crown of thorn,

"This woman whom I have loved with love supreme,
      Yet might not dream
Of kissing her pure garment's outmost seam,

"This woman, lo! she is mine, through many a year
        To hover near,
And passionately to worship, to revere!"

So I went viewless on the viewless air
        Fleetly to where
She sat in a green garden, calm and fair.

I clasped her with intangible arms like light,
        In fervid might,
And on her sweet proud beauty fed my sight!

I rained quick kisses on her lips and eyes,
        And loverwise
I sank on her deep bosom with deep sighs!

And she, meanwhile, with smooth lids drooping low,
        Chaster than snow,
Sat there superbly calm, and did not know!

My most impetuous kiss — the intense wild stress
        Of each caress —
Alike to her was an utter nothingness!

Cold pangs through all my ghostly being shot;
        I loathed my lot,
I that possessed and yet possessed·her not!

And now to God on every wind is borne
        My moan forlorn:
"Have pity, O God, and give me back her scorn!"

PEST.

I CAME at midnight to the city's great
    Last gate.

Below me gleamed its shadowy stately maze
    Of ways;

Domes, minarets, obelisks, firm-reared to dare
    Mid-air;

Masses of blended roofs in shadow deep
    As sleep;

And woven among its thousand streets and sites,
    Dim lights.

But now, as I bore onward to that great
    Last gate,

A dark shape stole toward me, glided fast
    And past.

With wonderment I turned, not trusting quite
    My sight,

When lo! the shape beneath me on the hill
    Stood still,

And even as I had turned, so turned apace
    Its face.

Wherewith the moon, from out a cloudy lair,
    Broke fair,

And showed me, lit with large eyes burning dull,
  A skull !

. . . .

Days after, this news reached me in the West:
  " The pest

"Sweeps Ispahan with its embittered breath
  Of death !

" Within the temples prayers and maddened cries
  Arise ;

" And by her heaps, forever newly fed,
  Of dead,

" Our city moans for Allah to disperse
  The curse."

WINE.

I AM a spirit strong and glad,
 In gold or purple proudly clad,
With eyes of fire and fragrant breath,
Lovely, but crueller than death !

Through days my protean soul has hung
In lucid clusters, richly strung
Through many a spacious green expanse
Of beauteous and historic France !

Below blue deeps of laughing skies
My soul has laughed, in soft surprise,
To hear what merry pleasure stirs
The voices of the vintagers !

But though at many a revel flit
The rapid javelins of my wit,
Though joy obeys me, though regret
May quaff my Lethe and forget,

Still do I love by stealth to wind
My subtle spells o'er heart and mind,
Till sacred secrets, treasured dear,
Are babbled in some greedy ear!

And I have loved to pluck aside
The mask from malice, envy, pride;
To strip fair flesh from deeds, and show
What bony motives grin below!

For when I cheer the kindliest him
Who courts me at his goblet's brim;
When I am blandest, warmest, then
Most deadly is my hate of men!

Nor is to me that moment sweet
When solemn mourners dumbly meet,
And dying lips are lifted up
To touch my sacramental cup, —

But keenlier does the moment please
If my drugged lover wakes and sees,
Like one who vaguely understands,
The red crime crusted on his hands!

TO-MORROW.

I SIT and muse beside the faded coals,
   While night and silence hold their mystic sway,
And while the world, with all its freight of souls,
   Wheels on through darkness to another day!

Across my spirit ghostly fancies creep . . .
   Who shall dare prophesy to-morrow's light?
What if uncounted thousands, while they sleep,
   Are trembling on eternity to-night?

And still they haunt my heart, these dreams forlorn,
   Vague bats of fear that sunshine would dismay . . .
Though myriads of to-morrows have been born,
   What if the last had perished with to-day?

But no! the ancient ordinance yet reigns . . .
   Hours afterward, while seated wakeful here,
I dimly see, along my casement-panes,
   The first pale dubious glimmerings appear.

Once more the old fated ways of earth begin . . .
   Some glad girl somewhere will soon wake and say,
While blushing from chaste forehead to sweet chin
   One lovely rose, — " It is my wedding-day!"

And in some prison-cell, perchance even now,
   Some haggard captive from his sleep is drawn,
To hear them, while cold sweat-drops bead his brow,
   Nailing a scaffold in the ghastly dawn!

DEGREE.

WHAT if the great earth where our life
    Appears so vast and fierce a strife,

Where mighty kingdoms rise and sink,
Where warriors fight, reformers think,

Where statesmen plot, where poets rave,
Where science makes the lightning slave,

Nay, what if all that meets our sight
In starry calms of utmost night,

All pale complexities we trace
In the awful altitudes of space,

All orbs among those baffling heights,
The suns of myriad satellites, —

What if all these and all they hold
Of lands and peoples manifold,

Were, to the eyes of one afar, —
One mortal as we mortals are, —

Like those mere giddy motes that dance
Within a sunbeam's lucid lance?

While he, in strange stupendous ways,
Lived on through monstrous nights and days,

Able, if chance might so allot,
To breathe us in and know it not!

THE ATONEMENT.

DULL as a withered flower, along the West,
    The sad moon dropt at dawn through brightening air,
And gazing on her calm and colorless breast,
    I marked the shadowy desolations there!

Then while the vanishing night grew more remote,
    Aided of some new sense, I seemed to hear
A voice of strange monotonous murmur float
    Miraculously down from that far sphere.

" Forever," the mysterious voice made moan,
    " I terribly expiate a mighty crime ;
I wander about this ghastly world alone,
    And shall be wandering till the end of time !

" No animate thing at all my sight beholds,
    No glimmer of any grass or sign of tree.
One monstrous lethargy of stagnation folds
    The appalling solitudes that compass me !

" Great valleylands in vapory distance die,
    Clammy with dews, with skull-shaped stones o'erstrewn,
And pale against the unchanging arch of sky
    Tower up these awful mountains of the moon !

And sometimes, journeying on with low-bowed head,
   I meet old bones that wondrous things avow
Of years before God touched this planet I tread
   With the woful death-in-life that shrouds it now!

" And often I so abhor this lonely lot
   That my sick spirit a keen delight would take
In seeing some white ghost haunt some dusky spot,
   Or setting a naked foot on some cold snake!

" But not even such poor boon I dare expect,
   While ever wandering through this loathsome land,
With hair and beard one tangle of red neglect,
   And thirty pieces of silver in my hand! "

TIGER TO TIGRESS.

THE sultry jungle holds its breath;
   The palsied night is dumb as death;
The golden stars burn large and bland
Above this torrid Indian land;
But we, that hunger's pangs distress,
Crouch low in deadly watchfulness,
With sleek striped shapes of massive size,
Great velvet paws and lurid eyes!

Hark! did you hear that stealthy sound
Where yonder monstrous ferns abound?
Some lissome leopard pauses there;
Let him creep nearer if he dare! . . .

And hark, again! in yonder grove
I hear that lazy serpent move;
A mottled thing, whose languid strength
Coils round a bough its clammy length!

Soon the late moon that crimsons air
Will fall with mellow splendors where
The Rajah's distant palace shows
Its haughty domes in dark repose.
And from this dim lair, by and bye,
We shall behold, against pale sky,
With mighty gorges robed in gloom,
The wild immense Himalayas loom!

At moonrise, through this very spot,
You still remember, do you not,
How that proud Punjab youth, last night,
Sprang past us on his charger white,
Perchance to have some fair hand throw
A rose from some seraglio? . . .
Well, if to-night he passes, note
My hot leap at his horse's throat!

JAEL.

Then Jael, Heber's wife, took a nail of the tent, and took a hammer in her hand, and went softly unto him, and smote the nail into his temples, and fastened it into the ground: for he was fast asleep and weary. So he died. — JUDGES, iv. 21.

PRAISE me with shawm and cymbal, chant my
fame,
Barak and Deborah, till the high Lord hears.
From Zaänáim, sounding along the lands,
Past Tabor even to Ephraim let the name
Of Jael, wife of Heber, echo in song.
Lo, I have merited the applauding voice
Of prophetess and conqueror; I have won
Justly my loud renown — and purchased it
With deep unspeakable heart-pangs of wild pain!

Praise me, and bid the people praise, and call me
Deliveress of Israel, having wrought
Death to the invincible and tyrannous.
Praise me that spared not, pitied not and smote;
Praise me that murdered righteously, that am
Glorious among all Hebrew womankind
For evermore. Praise me, yet praise aloof,
And hither send no curious messengers,
Bidding me join your jubilant sacrifice,
Your minstrelsy, your clamor of triumph. Close
I have drawn the curtains of my tent and shut
Heaven's vague supremities and the twilight moon,
Palm-gilding, from mine eyes. I would that doors

Of massive metal dulled your grateful songs
To me, lying prone, veiled with my loosened hair,
An agony in my thoughts and loathing life!

Have I not battled against my sin, O God,
And battled bravely? Father, am I not
Wrestler with that fierce passion which had coiled
About the immaculate column, fold by fold,
Of wifehood's beauteous chastity? Why, then,
Having so risen against myself and hurled
To the dust my baser part, can I not gain
Quiet of soul for recompense? O Lord,
Wherefore should this unholy love live on?
Whence this untamable longing to undo
Mine act?—this grief defiant of mastery?—
This weariness of self-hatred, whence, O Lord?

Nay, Father, have I once yielded to my love?
Did not my indignant spirit from the first
Cry out against it? Wakening after dreams
Of guilty impetuous worship, night by night
While Heber slept have I not stolen unheard
To part the tapestries, and gone forth and met
The large white stars of Israel, and made,
With suppliant arms and tears and back-thrown head,
Kneeling, my lamentation? Verily
Thou knowest, O God, I have done this thing; nay, too,
Thou knowest of how the quick pulse ruled my heart
When Sisera was near, yet how I have made
Face, form, and gesture one cold courtesy
Of decorous matronhood severely pure,
Acting until the last my virtuous lie,

Feeling the insolent animal in my veins
Gnaw at its bonds with fiery teeth. . . . And when,
Wounded and weak, I saw him stand to-day,
Bloody from horrible carnage, by the tent,
Thou knowest, O God, what yearning thrilled my breast
To hide, to save, even die befriending him;
Yet how with sternest afterthought I crushed
This eagerness. trampled, scorned it, and became
Guileful to bid him enter and fear not.

And yet Thou knowest, O Father, when he sank
Heavily on yonder couch of leopard-skins
And made his moan for water and turned his eyes
In pleading up to mine, how pity urged
My unwilling hands to kindly offices.
And then, and only then, for a little time
(Thou knowest, O God, 'twas but a little time!)
I served him, love being dominant, and stood
To watch him sleep tired sleep, athirst no more.
And then, and only then, for a little time,
(For a little time, O God, Thou knowest well!)
I fed the insatiate hunger of my look
With all his marvellous beauty, grace and strength:
The brow's white loftiness, the shadowing sweep
Of silken eyelash, the dark plenteous beard
Just curling about his grand firm-corded throat,
The vigorous majesties of girth and build
And eminent stature and heroic arms
And all that makes the manliness of a man!
For a little time, O God, for a little time! . . .
And then Thou knowest how sharp a serpent-sting,

After that one wild wanton moment, pierced
My bosom, and how I rose and hid my face,
Remembering I was Jael, mother and wife;
While to my ears the imagined mockery
Of those who might have spoken it, had they known,
Sounded: " Lo, she, the austerely blameless, loves
Jabin's dread captain, wronger of women, base,
Impious, a despot in the land!" . . .
                              Sing on,
Barak and Deborah, bless the Kenite's wife,
Who thrust the deadly nail in Sisera's brow,
Who strove to free not Israel, but herself.
Who failed, and feels the unholy love yet live,
And who now mourns the irreparable deed,
Lying prone in her self-hatred and despair!
O guessing not of her misery and shame,
Sing to her praise, flute-throated prophetess,
And thou, too, strong son of Abínoam, sing, —
While Jael hears, the accursed, the comfortless!

VIOLANTE.

(RAVENNA, A.D. 1500.)

The main incident of this poem has been suggested by Boccaccio, though it is said not to be of his invention. He has treated it in a comic manner, quite opposite to the one here employed.

LEAN closer yet, Fiametta. Catch my hand
Right firmly and hold it to your smooth cool palm,
Not mindful if the fever of it burn
Your clinging fingers, nor if spasms of pain
Jar it within your clasp. For a little space
Bear with me, *cara mia*, innocent one,
Just sixteen, with the great eyes and rich hair.
To-morrow, if you are leaning o'er my bed,
I shall be white and wordless, though you raved!

Oh, it is well they have not brought a priest!
Let them not bring one, for I truly fear
I should go mad and spit at him, once brought.
Fiametta, look you, I am wholly damned,
Steeped horribly in red sin past cleansing change,
Damned to the inmost core of this poor soul,
Streaked thick with guiltiest mirk from brow to heel,
Doomed and damned utterly! Child, it could avail
Nothing if I got holiest rites of church
At the last hour, being what I am. So, now,
Taunt me, I pray you, with no sight of priest!
Nay, only let me lie and brokenly gasp

In your alarmed ear this strange terrible tale
Of my supreme crime . . . Surely at its end
The effort will have left me power no more
Than just for one fleet farewell. After this,
Though a million organs groaned my requiem up
To high God through a million censers' fumes,
My spirit in anguish would be writhing still!

Lean closer yet, Fiametta . . . close, close, close!
Lean, though you loathe me when I have told you all
The appalling truth . . . What maiden more than I
Stood eminent for piety's eager zeal
In service of all reverent prayerful ways?
While Giulia wasted hours in how to make
The red flower glow its loveliest from her curls;
While plump Francesca strained the bodice-cord
To lend her opulent bust a prouder curve;
While gay Ninetta babbled of her loves,
And flashed from shadowing ambush a full smile
On many a passing gallant; while for these
The frivolous mood begot the flippant act,
And life went singing lightly, plume in cap, —
I always, I, Violante, thought no thought
That was not wed with Heavenly services,
Ave and fast and patient watch of self,
Penance, retirement, prayer, till people said
They looked to see the vague aureola rim
My tresses, and so crown me thoroughly saint!

Was not I pure, Fiametta? For you know
The unwearied worship that I poured like wine
Within my golden chalice of love to God!

Nor did one pulse of vanity stir my blood
When murmured praise for spotlessness divine
Met me and broke about me, wave on wave.
Nay, to mine ears that in devout dreams heard
The choric seraphim, all such praises came
Like echo of echo, meriting slight care.
For what to me the applausive heed of men,
The dross of mortal eulogy and the dust?
Alone desirable was Heaven, alone
Adorable the body and blood of Christ,
His grace of sheltering help, His peerless fame!

Lean close, lean close, Fiametta . . . Even as oil
Under the large serene flame of my faith,
Dwelt Guido's counsel, godlier, as it seemed,
For stainless vicarship of God on earth,
Than whatsoever man wore priestly guise,
In sanctitude of godliest office. Him
I held in hours confessional, or in hours
Of fervent pupilage, for a soul rare-graced
By strength and purity to meet the full
Bewildering glory of Heaven and falter not,
Weak-sighted for no qualms of timid shame.
He seemed the firm aerial stair that led
In stately spiral up to Heavenly peace. —
The voice wherewith God clothed His living thought,
His inexhaustible wisdom. Utter truth,
Chastity, eloquence, faith, sympathy,
Seemed wedded to all the man's least word or work,
Looked at me from his steadfast limpid eyes,
Made visible language of his white wide brow

Affirmed its kingly presence and calm power
By countless gentle and intangible ways,
That were not and still were, mysteriously!

He never gave me one faint flower of praise,
Just as he never, by one slight thorn of blame
Touched me, until that morning when I knelt
Before him in the solemn shadowy void
Of the still church. Then, even as one might say,
Right in my lap he dropt a marvellous bloom
Whose color and odor made me gasp for joy!

Lean closer yet, Fiametta . . . All that night
I lay awake and heard the inaudible
Darkness going past me as a great throng goes.
The ecstatic memory of Guido's words
To sweet monotony of low murmuring
Shaped itself, and with ever-visitant flow
Throbbed through the chamber's dumb tranquillity.
For hark you, he had told me I was beloved
Of Gabriel, God's best angel, and that he,
Even this same spirit of such high holiness,
Now yearned to assume what shape would least o'er-
 whelm
With its exceeding splendor these frail eyes,
And so make evident, past all dream of doubt,
The boundless honor of his angelic love!
Nay, too, in Guido's vision, as he said,
Were named the very place and hour whereat
This rare miraculous meeting should be held!

The place — that desolate ruin near the sea,
From whose gray vine-twined solitude one views

By a glance valleyward our placid town;
The hour — mid-watch on one of these late-past
Mild, lordly, and lucid nights of the June moon.
And I should await him there and then; and he
Would come (O passionate thought!) — would come to meet
Me, the elect, the all-favored, Violante,
Judged worthy in soul of high seraphic heed.
Yea, worthy as was that Thecla, she who made
The assailant beasts cower meekly while she stood
Naked in reach of their red rabid mouths.
Worthy as was Veronica, who bore
On virginal bleeding brows the thorn-crown's weight,
In beatific agony Heaven-conferred,
And bare on bosom and feet and hands through years
The five wounds of Christ's passion.
       Vanity!
Why, now, Fiametta, did I reek of it,
I, the calm mirror of whose guileless heart,
No tenderest breath of self-love ever blurred!
Oh, to my thought, until the Archangel kept
That bond of gracious deifying tryst,
All intermediate hours were shod with lead!
You are mindful yet, sweet sister, how I locked
My chamber, nor would open to any call?
You thought me prisoned thus for fast and prayer,
For rigor of solemn penance, nor once dreamed
'Twas vanity bade me dwell aloof that day!
Such vanity as had made me hold my face
Too sacred for your violative look,
Your touch of hands a soilure, and your chance words
An insolence . . . Oh, shame! unspeakable shame!

Noiseless and brave, on the next night, I stole
Forth from the dead-still house, and hurrying thence
Through many a moonlit street, got past the town
And gained the slumberous olive-slopes that led
By countless green gradations to the dark
Wreck of what once was haughtiest masonry.
The immense austere half-crumbled power of stone
Loomed vague in the wide wan moonlight. All the sea,
Beyond its marge of clear-cut prominent cliff,
Beamed like a pearl in luminous amplitude,
Save where one blaze of narrowing silver cleft
Its blue calm like a great fallen scarf of light.

Deep in the shadow of the ruin I plunged,
And waited, silent amid silence, then,
For what should follow, faithful every way
To Guido's charges . . . and at length I saw
A glimmer of white robes in the dubious dusk,
And heard the long sweet murmur "*Violante*,"
And knew the murmurer neared me with slow steps
Yet utterly soundless ; and at this I fell
Abject, being smitten to the bone with awe . . .

. . . .

Well, I have learned what Heaven means, Fiametta,
Eaten of it fruitwise, caught its keenest bliss,
Had it and held it just for a few fleet hours . . .
Now, as the price of this my arrogant gain,
(Since I, a mortal, have felt immortal joys)
Hell yawns to entomb me in its dread duress !

. . . .

I know not when, amid the ineffable
Delight of that sweet meeting, slumber came

To o'ermaster and annul my thought . . . I slept
Dreamlessly at the last, — then suddenly woke.

The ruin was bathed in dawn . . . I rose and stood
Beset with blithe tumultuous memories,
Till at my feet the gleam of a white robe drew
Both glad eyes eagerly groundward. One soft cry
Burst from my lips as kneeling I thought to see,
Clear under lavish light, the Archangel's face . . .
And saw instead (lean close, close, close, Fiametta,
For the room darkens grimly and swart shapes
Of devil and imp seem girding at me now,
There, here, and everywhere!) . . . I saw, instead,
Guido, abruptly wakened of my cry
From slumber . . . Guido, garbed with terrible art;
Guido, the man, — not Gabriel, the divine!

Ah, me! what incommunicable despair
Rushed on me then! He rose and widely spread
Both arms out toward me, but I shrieked and held
Before my fallen face two repelling hands,
While all the compassing morn seemed sown with cries
Of "Lost, lost, lost," from contumelious fiends;
And like the suddenness of a lightning-bolt
My infinite vanity and gross conceit,
The bold enormity of my utter crime
In having dared to esteem myself a soul
So exalted, flashed upon me! O the pang
Of that discovery! O the awful hate
Of self! the levelling overthrow! the shame!

I think you would have blushed to have called me pure
Ever at any time, had you but known

The curses I flung at Guido ere I turned
And left him grovelling for my pardon, prone
Reedwise before the tempest of my wrath!
Then hither I sped, and here through three wild days,
Three feverish days of torture, I have lain
And known that surely I am accurst beyond
All expiatory hope.   High up in Heaven,
How the chaste eyes of Gabriel must have blazed
Their holiest anger down on my vast guilt!
For what was I, a pitiable mean worm, —
Mean among loftier creatures, all most mean, —
That I should arrogate to my small poor self
Such wonder of gracious privilege, and trust
The all-worshipful would worship menial me?

I cannot feel your clasp, Fiametta, now,
Nor see your face except by fitful gleams,
Dead-pale, with tragic eyes and tremulous mouth.
They have won my soul, these fiends, and wait for it ...
The room is populous with them, and I breathe
Hot horrid waftures from their gibbering midst,
The sulphurous prelude of Hell's denser fumes.
Farewell, Fiametta ...   God be good to thee!
Fra Guido, I think, has hope of getting grace,
If he try hard, and shirk no pain of shrift.
Tell him I said he has not done monstrous wrong
Like me, being reverent all the while of him
Whose august name he used irreverently.
His sin was villanous brutal base deceit,
Lecherous and treacherous, an infamy!
But *mine* ...   Oh, God, the blasphemous egotism!
Farewell, Fiametta ...   I must pay its price!

MOZART'S REQUIEM.

A GLOOM had fallen upon great Mozart's life.
The spirits of wondrous melodies no more
Pleaded with his for animate being. Hope
Had suddenly fled, and melancholy stretched
Wide plumes of shadow above his daily dreams.
Fierce bodily pains had clutched him, and death's hand
Inexorably pointed to his grave.

In these dark hours, a stranger, tall, black-robed,
Sombre and pale of face, on a certain morn,
Glided across the threshold of his room,
Drew nearer, laid a purse of heavy gold
Before the astonished maestro, and at last
Broke silence with monotonous voice and sad.
" I have come," the stranger said, "to ask of you
The requiem for one loved, through lapse of years,
Beyond man's use, and bitterly mourned when dead.
Will Mozart weave its music, and create
Some passionate lamentation fit to seem
An utterance of unutterable grief?"

The maestro, drearily smiling, murmured, then:
" What time is given me to complete this dirge?"
" One month," was the answer. " Surely I could try,"
Mused Mozart, " yet success were doubtful hope."
Then, even as he had come, these few words said,
So noiselessly the stranger went.
                              Amazed,
Mozart long pondered in his mind these words,

Mysteriously communicate, till fire
Warmed his weak pulses, and the immortal rose
Within the mortal. Eagerness for the work
Possessed him, willing harmonies again
Rewandering all the labyrinths of his soul,
As suddenly over still enormous wastes
Of gale-abandoned forest wake once more
The old windy sounds, and lofty branches toss
The sleeping starlight from innumerous leaves !

With power and will and fervor he began
Fulfilment of his promise : but the month
Had passed not ere a violent malady
Seized his frail frame and forced him from the work.
And on the very morning that he rose,
Reprieved of death for a little longer, came
The stranger to demand the requiem.
" Nay, give me a second month," the maestro said,
" And if God spare me I shall keep my word.
Nobly begun, I would not hastily end
A work that lifts me to sublimest aims."

Whereat the stranger, with inscrutable face,
Cold, calm, unsympathetic, from beneath
His massive gloomy cloak drew forth a purse
Less heavy than the last, and slowly said :
" An hundred ducats I have given ; I give
For the added labor this half-hundred more ; "
And turning passed from the other's sight. But he,
Summoning a servant, bade him stealthily
Pursue the whither of this curious man ;
And while the servant sped to obey such hest,
In the brain of Mozart ghostly thoughts took shape.

And when the messenger brought back a tale
Of how he had followed with good zeal till soon
The stranger, at a crossing of two streets,
Abruptly had faded from his vigilance,
He knew not how — then Mozart's ghostly thoughts
Wore positive colors of conviction.   Strong
Within him was belief that he had seen
The presence of no earthly guest.   " I write,"
He would often murmur afterward, " the dirge
For mine own burial.   It is death's command!"

Exaltedly for days he strove to tell,
With eloquence of divinest cadences,
The infinite agony of some widowed heart
Mourning the irreparable.   His fine skill
Gathered all sorrowful sounds — wild chords or sweet,
Thrillingly plaintive peals, low interludes,
Ripples of light faint treble soft as tears,
And thunderous throbs of bass, to meet and form
One vast incomparable solemnity.
Genius had grown his vassal, while he toiled,
And beckoned him with beauteous hand where flew
The guiding glory of her white wings . . . till soon
In soft illimited amplitudes of dawn,
Glimmering she faded . . .
                        Now a darkness fell
Across the maestro's vision, and he lay
Incapable evermore, his high task done,
Having within its mighty music made
The unrivalled requiem of his own grand soul!

BEHIND HISTORY.

I AM the Queen they hold so pure.
　　They will carve my tomb one day, be sure,
With marble praise that shall endure.

I hear them bless me, low and loud;
The haughtiest head is bared and bowed
If I ride among the pressing crowd.

No churl of all my realm would tame
His hot hand should he hear my name
Called lightly by the lips of blame.

Many a life would proudly spill
Red loyal drops to work my will,
Or save me from one sting of ill.

Yet all the adoring care that I
Am guarded and am girded by,
Is reverence to a living lie! . . .

There served a man amid my train
Whom, day by day, with struggling pain,
I schooled my spirit to disdain.

A vassal base of birth was he;
And yet (ah, God! that it should be!)
His mere brute beauty maddened me.

For days, for weeks, I strove and prayed,
Loathing the strong strange love that weighed
On the white life it dared invade.

At last I wearied from my soul
Of endless effort to control
Desire that never gained a goal.

BEHIND HISTORY.

I laughed a reckless bitter laugh:
Lo, prayer was even as arid chaff,
And continence a shattered staff,

Since neither might avail to bring
Me any peace, or pluck the sting
From infinite pangs of coveting.

And so it fell, one fatal hour,
That passion burst, with sudden power,
To poisonous and full-petalled flower.

I met him in most secret wise . . .
Full presently from his mild eyes
Obeisance died and was surprise . . .

But after, in a little space,
It was with all his lit flushed face
As sudden morn in a dull place.

And watching him with wild unrest,
I saw his great mute joy confest,
And leaped toward his willing breast! . . .

* * * * * * * *

Now this was in the early night;
But when the first vague veil of light
Filmed heaven, he past from out my sight,

And groping down the palace-stair,
In the grey gloom met unaware
My masked assassin, crouching there! . . .

* * * * * * * *

I am the Queen they hold so pure:
They will carve my tomb one day, be sure,
With marble praise that shall endure!

THE STATUETTE.

YOU see that marble shape, so gay of mien,
 My lithe Terpsichore with the tambourine?

Last year in Paris, as you may have read,
A certain duke was murdered in his bed.

Deepest of secrets! No one knows to-day
Whose hand it was that smote him where he lay!

The heir sold all his grandeurs, piece by piece:
I bought this statuette out of pure caprice.

For just above the poor duke's bed, you see,
Hung bracketed this same Terpsichore.

And now I fancy that with each pure charm
Of dimpled cheek, blown hair, or curving arm,

Lies blent a shadowy fear, a faint distress,
That vaguely mars the sculptured loveliness.

And I, remembering that on one so gay
So grim a secret wearily must weigh,

Have sometimes dreamed that when the room is mute,
And clothed upon with darkness absolute,

Those bloodless marble lips will strangely stir,
And they that hunt the unpunished murderer,

Might hear, if through this dead-black room they came,
The low mysterious naming of a name! . . .

INDIVIDUALITY.

> Let it be remembered that, if individual life is short, the life of the human species is not short; its indefinite duration is practically equivalent to endlessness; and, being combined with indefinite capability of improvement, it offers to the imagination and sympathies a large enough object to satisfy any reasonable demand for grandeur of aspiration. — JOHN STUART MILL.

READING of radiant change, divine advance,
    Through all humanity's immense expanse,
At end of unknown ages vast in length,
With keen prophetic look I seemed to see
The miracle man's future fate would be,
    His lordly knowledge and transcendent strength!

I watched the race whence I myself had sprung
In vaguely distant days. while time was young,
    Now walk the astonished earth with godlike ease.
Nature, once ruling them, now owned their power,
And Science, pointing toward her proudest tower,
    Dropped humbly at their feet her golden keys!

I watched all varied tribes beneath the sun
Gather with lovely grandeur into one,
    And serve the nobler patriotism aright;
I saw the august unnavigable air
Wide-sown with buoyant barges everywhere,
    Majestic shapes by day, new stars by night!

Sly statecraft, greeds malign, hates lurid-eyed,
Crawled lamely into secret lairs and died,
   Blessing the wearied world with sweet release;
Dark broods of savage evils, near and far,
Cowered low at wisdom's gaze, and scowling war
   Wreathed her black guns with dewy blooms of peace!

I marked how some large purpose was fulfilled
That power supernal had sublimely willed;
   I marked, in thrilling vision, while I read,
How the full flower of manhood backward bore
From the white splendor of its dazzling core
   The last rich petal, and was perfected!

But through this dream of marvels that should be,
One strange sardonic thought came haunting me
   With the mute pathos of weak yearning tears:
In all such halcyon times what joy or pain
For him whose dust inertly shall have lain
   A nothingness through millions of slow years?

What message in this lofty cheerless creed
Aids personality's commandant need?
   What comfort in this cold imperious plan,
Where all men, whether ill or nobly wrought
Lie crushed beneath one awful Juggernaut,
   The universal commonweal of man!

The love, hate, hope, fear, passion that is I,
The throbbing self that loathes to wholly die,
   Disdains a future where it holds no place,
As one with lot beside the Euphrates cast
Might carelessly disdain that stately past
   When Babylon's domes dared heaven, in mighty
     grace!

ORDER.

LIKE skeletons rise the bare trees, gaunt and stark;
  The poignant air is calm; no breezes roam;
Millions of stars pierce the blue winter dark,
  And fill with throbbing radiance its deep dome.

I throw my head far backward till there stay
  No gleams of earth in what my vision meets,
And through night's luminous blooms I seem to stray,
  As through a summer meadow of marguerites!

At the grand order of this intricate maze,
  Its boundless balance, its miraculous art,
I thrill with wonder that no words can phrase . . .
  Yet a strange thought strikes discord through my
    heart!

What if some portion of this awful plan
  Grew suddenly weak and faltered in its place,
And one long mighty ominous shudder ran
  Through all the immense black altitudes of space?

And satellite planets from their own suns fled,
  To plunge amid cold voids of skies unknown,
With all the peoples upon their bosoms dead,
  And all their haughtiest cities overthrown?

And system told to system its wild fears,
   Till each in fiery disarray was riven,
And terrible crashes of colliding spheres
   Roared ruin through the infinitudes of heaven!

. . . .

Dizzied and shocked at my own ghastly dream,
   Again toward earth I turn my dazzled sight,
And watch how tranquilly the dim lands gleam,
   Touched by the grave quietus of the night!

Filled with new thoughts, on heaven once more I gaze,
   And hear, while peace restores me to her spell,
Invisible sentinels down starry ways
   Pass the deep resonant watchword, "*All is well!*"

CONCEPTION.

"In its ultimate essence nothing can be known."
                         HERBERT SPENCER.

I CLOMB a great height in a dream;
   To lordlier reaches I attained,
Till even the uttermost I gained,
   Serene, supreme.

There fell from off mine eyes, at this,
   The dimming scales of sense. I saw
Matter, unleashed from every law,
   That which it is.

And real at last and face to face,
    Marvels that no man could forget,
    The mighty mysteries I met
        Of Time and Space.

Or yet I followed, course by course,
    Like one that deals with tangled skeins,
    The intricate interblending veins
        That flow from Force.

Till now the shadow across me came
    Of something soon to burst in light;
    A hope, a wonderment, a fright
        I dared not name!

And then, as though some signal nod
    Bade that the utmost be revealed,
    I reeled with awe, and, while I reeled,
        Thought this thought: *God!*

FAME.

I SAW in dreams a long and wavering way
    That wound and wound toward the walls of day.
Like a great snake on a wide moor it lay.

At either road-edge there were men who kneeled,
Some with bowed countenances half revealed,
Some crying drearly, some whose lips were sealed.

Ill might you say what presence or what thing
They waited, in their watchful cowering,
As suppliants wait the advent of a king.

And now there moved a murmur through them all,
For a vast shape, fantastically tall,
Came gliding on, with pace majestical.

In shadowy and indeterminate wise
Fluttered the mistlike draperies of its guise;
Its face was vaguely stern, with scornful eyes.

In either hand it carried bounteous bays,
Wrought greenly into wreaths of braided sprays,
As were the old chaplets of the dead Greek days.

And wheresoe'er that journeying spirit came,
They caught his vaporous robe, they wailed his name,
While many a faded face was touched with flame.

But rarely, very rarely, he bent down,
Mixed with a languid smile his august frown,
And dropt on some low brow a glimmering crown.

Then, just as my strange dream was like to cease,
His face drew near, and on its haughty peace
I read unbounded tyranny of caprice!

CRITICISM.

"CRUDE, pompous, turgid," the reviewers said.
   "Sham passion and sham power to turn one sick!
Pin-wheels of verse that sputtered as we read —
   Rockets of rhymê that showed the falling stick."

A would-be murderer cannot always kill;
   Some missiles leave some shields without a dint.
That book was loved, against the critics' will,
   By those who do not put their love in print.

But while, assaulted of this buzzing band,
   The poet quivered at their little stings,
White doves of sympathy o'er all the land
   Went flying with his fame beneath their wings!

And every fresh year brought him love that cheers,
   As Caspian waves bring amber to their shore;
And it befell that after many years,
   Being now no longer young, he wrote once more.

"Cold, classic, polished," the reviewers said.
   "A book you scarce can love, howe'er you praise.
We missed the old careless grandeur as we read —
   The power and passion of his younger days!"

ATTAINMENT.

I SHAKE the dusty film inaction weaves
   Round this old volume, shelved in closet-glooms,
And while I slowly turn its yellowing leaves,
   I seem as one within a place of tombs!

For all the book, unread so long, so long,
   Breathes deeply of forgotten dreams . . . and lo!
From out its pages drops the little song
   I made in callow boyhood, years ago!

It seems to-day so slight and weak indeed,
   That little song which once I toiled to make,
And yet the trivial stanzas, while I read,
   Low sweet memorial echoings awake!

Surely, stray waif, you do me grievous wrong, —
   Me, having won a fame to shine and last!
'Twere wise if I should burn you, little song,
   Poor fragile faded violet of the past!

But ah! to feel the old fervors I have felt
   In days ere Art bowed humbly to my kiss,
When spurned, although adoring still, I knelt,
   Yet paid no worship worthier than was this!

O dearer far than song's divinest might
   The aspiring voice that falters while it sings!
And lovelier than all lordliness of flight
   The wingless impotence that yearns for wings!

A KING.

(A certain mood of a certain mind, contemplating death.)

IT is more than being great
   At the random rule of fate,
To lie as he lies here,
Very awful and austere.
'Tis more than being wise
To repose with placid eyes,
And know not of the wild world that it cries, cries,
   cries!

Look ye now, and answer true
If it be as well with you,
That fret and sweat and sin
For the flesh ye weary in,
As with him that bates his breath
And what empty words it saith,
To attain the life diviner, which is death, death, death!

What of pleasure shall he miss,
With that sovereign ease of his?
What of pain shall reach his ken,
With that marble scorn of men?
Though ye praised him in a psalm,
Though ye smote him of your palm,
Shall ye call him from this haughty sleep and calm,
   calm, calm?

Lo, his dumb face turns ye dumb
If to look on him ye come,
Who hath found in cold eclipse
A superb Apocalypse!
Who has had the last bad thing
The deciduous days may bring,
Who is crowned as none but Death could crown him,
    king, king, king!

WINDS.

O INVISIBLE lives, that aimlessly
    With mutable voices fare
Mysteriously and tamelessly
    Through the altitudes of air,
When I welcome lofty dreams of you,
    Amid hours of calms or storms,
I discern evanescent gleams of you
    As divine phantasmal forms!

Where dim skies vaguely illuminate
    Some remote unearthly reach,
You despond, rejoice or ruminate,
    You are low or loud of speech.
With murmurs that rise altisonant,
    Or with dreary moans, you meet;
With imperious uproars dissonant,
    Or melodies wildly sweet!

Here grouped in superb frigidity,
    The blasts of the North repose,
Proud spirits of stern intrepidity,
    Whose wings with clangors unclose.

In their saturnine eyes crepuscular
  Cold hatreds bitterly glow;
In the girth of their dark arms muscular
  Lie shipwreck, ruin and woe!

Here crouch like implacable savages
  Those gales of the East that bear,
With reckless calamitous ravages,
  The weight of the world's despair.
Grim sisters, gloomily cowering,
  They sing, in their cruel scorn,
Of ocean-waves vastly towering,
  And trees by the roots uptorn!

Here, clothed in raiments ethereal,
  The West winds roam and recline,
Diaphanous girls, with aerial
  Embraces that intertwine.
Their shapes have the fragile slenderness
  Of wheat, with its changeful lights,
And their eyes hold the mellow tenderness
  Of moons amid harvest-nights!

But near them, in easy reach of them,
  The winds of the warm South float,
Voluptuous beauties, with each of them
  ˙A wine-red rose at her throat!
The folds of their tresses are pillowing
  Large blooms of delicious balms,
And they sing of the long seas billowing
  On shores that are plumed with palms!

Thus, haughty in dread immobility,
   Or lurid in arrogant might,
Exultant in soft volatility,
   Or languid in drowsy delight,
Sublimely, serenely or dismally,
   Weird throngs, you glimmer and go,
Where spaciously loom and abysmally
   The realms that my visions know!

THE COMET.

LONG ages, with slow change of regions and races
   Through all the proud breadths of this planet-sown sky,
Have fled since God fashioned, to roam its great spaces,
   This fiery grandeur and speed that is I.
He dowered my frame with a vigor that urges
   Its obdurate heart in unwearying flight;
He robed me with vapor whose luminous verges
   Trail wide on the dark awful hollows of night!

But ever before me, in dubious distance,
   Among dread dominions that stellar throngs fill,
Through breathless inanimate voids whose existence
   Looks one solemn nothingness frigid and still,
A spirit flies on where the gloom spreads immensely,
   Her garments like mine in pale splendor outflung,
Unseen save by perishing gleams yet intensely
   Adored of my soul since creation was young!

One loath to be loved, irresponsive, unheeding;
   One swayed by deep fervor and eager appeal;
One ever with fugitive brilliance receding,
   One following always with radiant zeal.
For æons untold we have ceaselessly darted
   Where vacancy's torpors of blackness lie mute,
Together, yet millions of mighty leagues parted,
   A terrible flight, an appalling pursuit!

Past intricate systems that view me in wonder
   And put with their brightness my own beams to scorn;
Through tracts where the volleying asteroids thunder;
   Past nebulous orbs that are yet to be born.
By suns that in richest of colors throb vivid,
   Or blaze with twin glory, star thrilling to star;
By ruins of old worlds burnt sickly and livid,
   Her misty magnificence guides me afar!

Some globes, ever flaming in hot conflagration,
   Give forth deadly blasts from their lurid red hells;
O'er some broods the curse of severe desolation,
   Of stagnant repose where no living thing dwells;
In some there are monsters whom nature has given
   Strange horrors of outline terrific to see;
Some hang like vast tears dropping always through heaven,
   From pole unto pole shoreless volumes of sea!

In some I behold haughty palaces tower;
   In some are low caverns of rough-shapen clay;
Some bear noble cities of opulent power;
   Some bear cities rotting in slothful decay;

In some there are creatures crime-soiled beyond telling;
    In others, where life wins its loftiest goal,
With stately tranquillity mortals are dwelling,
    Like gods in their beauty, and stainless of soul!

But while through celestial infinitudes fleeting,
    Along these weird courses enormous in scope,
Of golden attainment and rapturous meeting
    I dare not to question — I dare but to hope!
The drift of God's purpose, obscure past all seeing,
    What voice of what prophet hath spoken or sung?
And so in blind passion I chase this wild being,
    Adored of my soul since creation was young!

THE ICEBERG.

WHERE the keen wan peaks, in frigid pride unbending,
    Jut up against the abysmal blue of night;
When the red aurora, at the world's wild ending,
    Opens in heaven its awful fan of light,
A part of all the inviolate peace around him,
    Calm amid mighty quietudes did he rest,
The fierce cold for a manacle that bound him,
    The arctic stars to sparkle on his crest.

Here silence, like a monarch, reigned immensely,
    The quintessence of cold was here, no less,
Each utter as before God spake intensely
    And visible things leapt out from nothingness.

A land wherewith no living sign was blended,
    A white monotony of weird device;
One towering boreal torpor, chaste and splendid,
    One monstrous immobility of ice!

But when light woke within that bleak heaven, grandly
    To illume pale polar summits, range on range,
Then blindly through his glacial soul yet blandly
    He felt the movement of mysterious change.
He seemed to have heard across vast ocean-reaches
    A summoning voice from equatorial calms,
From languorous tropic bowers and lucid beaches,
    From blossoming headlands and high plumes of palms!

A voice compelling and a voice commanding,
    Yet sweet as flute-notes near still purple seas,
Strange beyond speech and strong beyond withstanding,
    Yet soft withal as tremulous airs in trees.
A voice of such deep charm that while he wondered
    Plungingly seaward his huge frame he bent,
And all its proud enormity was sundered
    From all its fetters of encompassment.

Then he went down superbly over distance
    Of mad uproarious surges, height on height,
That hurled tempestuous onslaughts of resistance
    Round his serene magnificence of might.
Then he went down across the unknown sea-spaces,
    A spot of radiance on their billowy whirl,
Scintillant with the sun's most dazzling graces,
    Or touched by moonbeams to phantasmal pearl!

One chill wind, like a breath of death, ran blowing
   Incessantly along his path austere,
And far before the grandeur of his going,
   Like birds the little vessels fled in fear.
Green flashed the glassy bastions whence transcendent
   His frosted pinnacles blazed out above,
While in colossal crystal calm resplendent,
   Superbly he went down to meet his love!

But journeying thus, too thrilled for all confusion
   Of boisterous wave or bluff blast to annoy,
He had lessened with insidious diminution,
   He had wasted and not known it in his joy.
For through him there had pulsed a fire of yearning
   'Twas ruin although 'twas rapture to have known,
And love within his frozen life lay burning,
   Like a ruby under fathoms of stern stone!

And so while passion in his dumb breast kindled
   A lordlier larger impulse to adore,
The more his eminent glories waned and dwindled
   As that ethereal voice allured the more.
And then with bitterest pangs he felt the fleeting
   Of all his luminous loftiness and pride,
And shuddered with the dark thought of not meeting
   That vague invisible love before he died!

And still the summoning voice came sweet and eager,
   Though touched with semitones of divine regret,
And hourly growing meagre and more meagre,
   He journeyed on, desiring, yearning yet! . . .
Till now he vanished utterly, and the tender
   Lulled waves of tropic ocean smiled above
Him that in all the morning of his splendor
   Superbly had gone down to meet his love!

PERSPECTIVES.

How much in life we utterly forget!
   How many pangs, how many smiles and tears!
What joy, what pain, what yearning, what regret
   Lies lost within the oblivion of dead years!

And journeying on, inexorably fast,
   Accomplishing our fated length of days,
We turn to look upon the ample past,
   Clothed bafflingly with indeterminate haze!

Its tracts of shadowy vagueness die away
   To meet the shadowy sky-line of all thought;
Dreamily neutral, featurelessly gray,
   They are not something, neither are they naught!

But here and there, in such clear-seen relief
   As scarce the annulling distance may efface,
We mark the rigid outline of some grief,
   Like a great tree that overtops its race!

Or yet like quiet hills, not towering high,
   Though proudly rounded, we discern, no less,
Joys that with beauteous dominance defy
   These ghostly vapors of forgetfulness!

But ah, how lovelier when our eyes have won,
   August in retrospect as we recede,
Like some snow-crested mountain bathed in sun,
   The pure firm grandeur of some noble deed!

THE MOON IN THE CITY.

PALE roamer through the purple hollow of night,
    In all thy wanderings weird from East to West,
What wonder thou dost gladly shower thy light
    On many a dusky region of earth's breast?

Wide tracts of cloisteral forest-land, I know,
    Are welcome to that luminous heart of thine,
Where under murmurous branches thou canst throw
    Dim palpitant arabesques of shade and shine!

Smooth meadows dying against far opal skies
    Thou lovest with lonely splendors to illume,
And turn their bodiless vapors, when they rise,
    To phantoms greatening in the doubtful gloom!

The haughtiest mountain happy dost thou feel
    To mantle with thy radiance, chastely soft,
Like intercessional mercy's meek appeal
    Where cold majestic justice towers aloft!

When deep in measureless peace he lulls his waves,
    Or when their perilous masses proudly curl,
Thy pennon of brilliance, though he smiles or raves,
    Along the varying sea dost thou unfurl!

But ah! though forest, mountain, meadow and sea
    Shall each thy separate favor sweetly win,
White lily of heaven, how can it pleasure thee
    To blossom above the city's ghastly sin!

FIRE.

For all that lives I am a spirit of hate;
  All beauty and strength I would annul or ban;
And yet, through some imperious edict, fate
  Puts my vast power within the rule of man.

For me, to whom sad ruin and death are sweet,
  This lowly slavery galls with pangs austere;
I loathe the illumined hearth where loved ones meet,
  The shivering outcast whose chilled frame I cheer.

In the wide hurry and clash of this great town,
  I long perpetually, with zeal intense,
To break the tyrannous bonds that bind me down
  And revel awhile in red magnificence!

Thus with invisible wrath I chafe and strain
  Amid my stern captivity's dreary days,
Till after infinite effort I attain
  A riotous liberty, and madly blaze.

Then in high watch-towers bells are tolled with might,
  And summoning peals ring loud above my roar,
And bold men with my turbulent fury fight,
  Till, utterly quelled, I am a slave once more!

But often amid defeat a thought that charms,
  While yet the water drowns my crackle and hiss,
Is that I have wrapped some life in these wild arms,
  Or laid on some dead face my blackening kiss!

DECAY.

WITH beauty and health and hardiness it shares
    Enduring sovereignty malign and strange ;
Innumerable are all its haunts and lairs ;
    Immeasurable its vast and stealthy range.

Forever varying in its forms of ill,
    Forever does it borrow, of stores immense,
Those opulent colors that await its will,
    Sombrely rich or radiantly intense.

On pools of foul miasmatic stagnance brood
    Its gentler tints of violet or of rose ;
Through many a wood's majestic solitude,
    In ruin of rotting logs its crimson glows.

Its mellower browns in faded blooms are seen ;
    Its rancorous yellows in slow rust exist ;
In noisome mildew lurks its pestilent green ;
    Its ghostly grays are in malarial mist.

In noxious mold are hidden its ashy blues ;
    Its ambers are in old marble's crumbling slabs ;
On desolate tombstones are its grimmer hues,
    Blots of dense black, or sullen-glimmering drabs.

But all its gaudier splendors full to air
    In Autumn's blighted foliage are outrolled,
And often amid sweet sunsets it will wear
    Deep melancholy purple or vivid gold !

Yet ah ! the agony that no words may speak,
   When, positive though intangible, it lies
In the red hectic flower on some dear cheek,
   Or shines with ominous fire from worshiped eyes !

Oh, then what wonder if our difficult lives
   Guess vaguely, from the shadow of their dim lot,
How some white incorruptibility thrives
   In luminous bournes of peace, where time is not ?

WASTE.

DOWN the long orchard-aisles where I have strolled,
   On fragrant sward the slanted sunlight weaves,
Rich-flickering through the dusk of plenteous leaves,
Its ever-tremulous arabesques of gold !

In globes of glimmering color, sweet to see,
   The apples greaten under halcyon sky,
   Green, russet, ruddy, or deep-red of dye,
Or yellow as the girdle of a bee !

But o'er the verdure's blended shine and shade
   Small blighted fruits lie strown in dull array,
   Augmenting silently from day to day,
Gnarled and misshapen, worm-gnawed and decayed.

And over them, as favoring sunbeams bless,
   To fair perfection will those others grow,
   In mellow hardihood maturing slow, —
While these will shrivel into viewlessness !

Ah, me! what strange frustration of intent,
  What dark elective secret, undescried,
  Lives in this dreary failure, side by side
With opulence of full-orbed accomplishment!

O seeming mockery! O strange doubt wherein
  The baffled reason gropes and cannot see!
  If made at all, why only made to be
In irony for that which might have been?

Nay, vain alike to question or surmise! . . .
  There, plucking white moon-daisies, one by one,
  Through yonder meadow comes my little son,
My pale-browed hunchback, with the wistful eyes!

DECORATION DAY.

TO-DAY, as the pulses powerful
  Of the glad young year awake,
It would seem that with tokens flowerful
  A nation had gone to take,

While passing in throngs processional
  Over sweeps of mellowed sod,
The sky for a blue confessional,
  And to tell its grief to God!

But more than to march regretfully
  With the earthward-pointing gun,
And more than to merge forgetfully
  The Blue and the Gray in one,

Were to love, with its sweet sublimity,
    The thought of an endless peace,
And to swear, in grand unanimity,
    That war shall forever cease !

For how is your service beautiful,
    O mourners that meet to-day,
If the hands that are now so dutiful
    Shall to-morrow spoil and slay ?

If the hate that your love is levelling
    Shall to-morrow lift its brow,
And redden with bloody revelling
    The graves that you garland now ?

For only if all humanity
    Could have learned to well abhor
The imperious blind insanity,
    The iniquitous waste of war,

Would the splendid and stainless purity
    Of to-day beam out afar,
Down the duskiness of futurity,
    As with light of a morning-star !

And then would the blooms you shed upon
    These numberless grave-mounds, be
As though the dews they had fed upon
    Were the waters of Galilee !

MAY 31st, 1875.

CUSTER.

(July, 1876.)

WELL had he won the honoring love we gave
    His resolute martial heart, to fear unknown,
Now lying at rest within his distant grave
    Beside the myriad-cañoned Yellowstone.

A spirit of splendid nerve to coolly dare ;
    Stern as an enemy, as a friend most true,
Impetuous, haughty, gallant, debonair ;
    Now fierce as fire and now as soft as dew,

In this adventurous life did we behold,
    Translated to those perilous lands afar,
The prowess of some new D'Artagnan, the bold
    Invincibility of some new Bayard !

May the rich picture that his memory leaves
    Light history's page for many an unborn year,
While many an unborn soldier proudly weaves
    Fresh laurels for this valorous cavalier !

Time the sweet radiance of his fame shall prove,
    And, while the unmeasured future flows along,
His sinewy figure, buckskin-clad, shall move
    Down glimmering paths of story and of song !

For horror thrills through every class and clan
    When wrong so riots in victory, and when
One in such eminent lordliness a man
    Lies ruined by these red mockeries of men !

So from thy sorrowing country thou shalt win
   Rank beside all her loyalest and her best,
Thou new Leonidas, with thy noble kin,
   Dead in that wild Thermopylæ of the West!

CUBA.

WE know the black scowl of her brow,
   Her tyrant greed, her bigot glee,
Old arrogant Spain, that reaches now
   A lean dark arm across the sea!

"Once slave, and so for ever slave,"
   On ocean-winds her proud words float,
While, by the warm Caribbean wave,
   Her talons meet in Cuba's throat!

And Cuba, levelled of the grip,
   Shivers and strains and fights to rise,
Her own blood on her moaning lip
   And anguish in her lurid eyes!

But clear, below that tropic sun,
   Gleams the wild hand she stretches forth,
Where the dim domes of Washington
   Bulge up against the mighty North!

And we, that know and hear and see
   Her strife to break from crushing powers,
To gain our giant help and be
   A thing no more that quails and cowers,

We hold her as some mere hurt brute,
  And muse, while watching her mad pain,
"Tobacco ... sugar ... coffee ... fruit ...
  She never should belong to Spain!"

JANUARY, 1873.

ALBERT F. WEBSTER, JR.

(DIED AT SEA, DEC. 27, 1876.)

LIKE a dreary wanderer, from the West,
  This tale of your lonely death departs,
And finding those who have loved you best,
  Knocks loud at the doorway of their hearts!

Our fears had faded; our hope re-bloomed;
  You had cheered us happily from afar;
Your danger seemed from the life it gloomed
  To pass like a cloud from the morning-star!

But yearning still for the sun that shines
  With a richer gladness on summer calms,
You sailed from the dark balsamic pines
  For blue Oceania's island-palms!

But while you were sailing, brief and stern
  Came the solemn summons that none can brave,
And now you rest, as in grief we learn,
  With the vast Pacific for your grave!

O friend, endowed with a worth so rare,
  Whom intellect served, whom truth obeyed,
O forehead so chastely, brightly fair
  With the shining aureole genius made!

What fatal irony follows man
    With a curse no wisdom hath understood,
And reels amid nature's ordered plan
    Like a drunken faun through a peaceful wood?

Should life, in its meagre and troublous term,
    Be marred by mockeries harsh as those
That set in the leaf's young green a worm,
    That kill in the bud its waiting rose?

That smite the lark as its wings unfold
    In the dawn whose thrilling dews they crave,
That shatter the column ere it hold
    The sculptured grace of its architrave?

Ah, proud philosophy, shut thy book!
    Art thou better, for all thy boasted might,
Than a little child, when it turns its look
    On the silver labyrinths of the night?

Ah, haughty science, whose hand can weigh
    The monstrous planet in mighty skies,
Thou hast not strength in thine arm, this day,
    To tear the bandage from off thine eyes!

. . . .

Yet, precious friend, into distance past,
    All Godlike mercy can only seem,
All sweet intuitions, first and last,
    Are wild delusion, are baseless dream,

Or still, dear lost one, your soul endures,
    High-sheltered from earthly cares and fears,
While brows that are more divinely yours
    Bend down in pity upon our tears!

TO EDWIN BOOTH.

On his Return to the American Stage.

DEATH, shadowing for a time thy future, leaves
    Its heaven unclouded, and the applausive throng
Gathers again where pale Melpomene weaves,
    In statuesque attitude austerely sweet,
    Still lordlier laurel-chaplets, fresh and strong,
    For him who walks again, with reverent feet,
Through stately lands of loved Shakspearian song!

As Denmark's prince we shall behold thy face
    Lighten or gloom in passionate change once more ;
Watch thee, with calm and meditative pace,
    Move toward the gates of death, to pause afraid !
    Or, like some terrible angel, stand before
        The cowering queen ; or meet thy father's shade
Among the moon-bathed towers of Elsinore !

Marvels of falsehood in the Moor's thrilled ear,
    As subtle Iago thou shalt softly sigh,
And be, while thy swart victim quakes to hear,
    The appalling incarnation of deceit,
    Untruth's transcendent charlatan, vastly sly,
    Snakily cunning, loathsomely discreet,
With lean dead smile and cold metallic eye !

And we shall watch ambition's fiercest fang
    Gnaw thee as Cawdor's throne-aspiring thane ;
Hear, in the witches' vault, thy footstep clang ;
    See thee, at gory Banquo's grim rebuff,
    Shackled with guilty horror's iciest chain ;
    Or, under that hot falchion of MacDuff,
Die like a slaughtered bull, at Dunsinane !

In these, and many immortal moods like these,
  May wondering thousands, with delighted care,
Note thy chaste charms of classic-postured ease,
    Thy sculptural face, thy rich voice, nor forget
  That thou of Kean, Macready and all who wear
    The buskin grandly in art's annals yet,
Beamest the radiant equal and true heir!

OCTOBER, 1873.

THE SCHOLAR'S SWEETHEART.

ALL day he toils, with zeal severe,
  On something learnedly polemic;
From Harvard he returned last year,
  With bounteous honors academic.
His parents name him but in praise,
  His little sisters quite adore him,
And all the loving household lays
  Allegiance willingly before him!

What forms his labor, week by week?
  They could not understand — oh, never!
'Tis something eminently Greek,
  'Tis something intricately clever!
But still his task, unfinished yet,
  He shapes with industry unflagging,
And writes his treatise that shall set
  The heads of noted pundits wagging!

Is it of Homer's doubtful lines?
  Or yet some question, subtly finer,
Of whether certain famous wines
  Were first obtained from Asia Minor?

Is it of dialects impure?
  Is it some long-fought rule of grammar?
Is it old Sanscrit roots obscure?
  Is it that wearisome digamma?

But whether this or whether that,
  Through fragrant fields, when work is ended,
While darkly wheels the zigzag bat
  And all the West is warmly splendid,
He steals to meet, in loving wise,
  With eager steps that do not tarry,
A rosy girl whose shining eyes
  Grow tender as she calls him "Harry."

What altered thoughts can she awake,
  This pearl of sweethearts, best and fairest!
And what a contrast does she make
  To 'comments on the Second Aorist'!
So strongly round him can she throw
  Her dazzling spells of sweet retention,
'Tis doubtful now if he could go
  Correctly through his first declension!

For while near mossy meadow-bars,
  With spirit thrilled by sacred pleasures,
He lingers till the dawn of stars,
  He lingers by the girl he treasures,
This grave young scholar scarcely knows
  If Hector was a fighting seaman,
If lofty Pindar wrote in prose,
  Or Athens lay in Lacedaemon!

LA BELLE HÉLÈNE.

I SAT in my small *loge*, five francs' worth,
   At the *Variétés*, unknown, ignored,
And heard, in its mad Parisian mirth,
   How the thousand-throated audience roared.

With all its volatile rompish glee,
   Do I often view that gay play yet,
As when, a wave in the living sea,
   I stared at the stage through my good lorgnette.

It was travesty under its wildest spell,
   It was sad Melpomene, grand, serene,
With her stately peplum tucked up well,
   To frolic in French *à la Colombine*.

The *Belle Hélène* — who has forgotten it?
   That mass of incongruous lights and shades —
That making a new French roof to sit
   On the Parthenon's haughty colonnades!

That blending of most antipodal things —
   Old reverend Homer stretched on the rack —
Sublime Agamemnon, a king of kings,
   Keeping time to the tunes of Offenbach!

The mighty Achilles made to forget
   Both prince and demigod in a trice,
And Calchas, the awful soothsayer, set
   To playing at " Goose " with loaded dice !

It is all so droll that my lips, I know,
   Give lusty share to the laughter brave ;
But my mirth has a mournful thought below,
   Like the darkness under a sparkling wave !

I remember the dead heroic days,
   The reckless sin of the Spartan wife,
The black ships thronging the blue sea-ways,
   And the ten wild stubborn years of strife !

I think of how many solemn scenes
   In that old majestic story dwell ;
Of slaughtered heroes and weeping queens,
   Of woful appeal and wailed farewell !

I see Andromache strive to check
   The tears from a soul that sorrow racks,
With one white arm about Hector's neck
   And one round the babe, Astyanax.

I see, at the fatal fearful hour,
   Pale Iphigeneia wait to die ;
Or Helen stands on the Scæan tower,
   And curses life with a bitter sigh.

Cassandra, crying her people's doom,
   Disdained of those that should heed her most ;
Lonely Penelope, at her loom,
   On desolate Ithaca's gray coast.

And saddest of all, in pathos sweet,
  Old white-haired Priam, a suppliant one,
Low-bent at the proud Pelides' feet,
  To beg the corpse of his dearest son!

So these and so other legends kept
  The feet of memory wandering slow
Near the hearts that throbbed and the eyes that wept
  Two thousand shadowy years ago!

And I said to myself, "Those tricks of song,
  Those *can-can* follies that half appall,
Those odd buffooneries, witty and wrong,
  Are sorry ways to remember it all."

"And yet," I mused, "it is surely best
  That the meanest weed on a grave should grow
Than that barren sods lie above the rest
  Of the crumbling slumberer below!

"And here on this busy and fickle earth,
  It were wiser, doubtless, did one confess
Even such sham memories more of worth
  Than voids of utter forgetfulness!"

GENTLEMAN JO.

IN the years of youth, ere the years despoil,
    When death is a word we seldom say,
    When the Hebe of health pours wine all day
And the lamp of life burns odorous oil,
    Oh, sweet to clasp, and to clasp anew,
    One friend by the hand whose heart rings true,
And glows with your own lost love's rare glow,
    Gentleman Jo! Gentleman Jo!

I see your eyes, of a brown so warm,
    Your deep sweet dimples, your tossed brown hair,
    Your easeful gracious courteous air,
And the strong fine curves of your manful form.
    Not a hint of the clever stuff you wrote
    In trick of collar, caprice of coat, —
Not a touch of the false, the flippant, no!
    Gentleman Jo! Gentleman Jo!

Was there ever a man as keen as you
    To strip all sham of its gaudy guise?
    To aim your scorn upon social lies
And with shafts of laughter shoot them through?
    When your cheek flushed up with the circling
        cheer,
    What a happy thing was your voice to hear,
In its rhythmic richness, loud or low,
    Gentleman Jo! Gentleman Jo!

Yet you dealt in nothing to flash and fade,
  No smart grandiloquence mock-sublime,
  No dainty curse of the men, the time,
No brilliant brummagem of tirade;
  No flimsily-dazzling cynic trope,
  Where the egotist hides in the misanthrope;
Not the least word meant for mere bald show,
    Gentleman Jo! Gentleman Jo!

For the love was large in your breast innate,
  Your charity mild as a mother's tears;
  When you flung at the world your trenchant
      sneers
It was duty spoke, it was never hate!
  And the blows were struck with a better nerve,
  Since the hand that gave them was fain to serve;
Would have rather blest than have struck one blow,
    Gentleman Jo! Gentleman Jo!

You counted the petty spites and greeds
  That buzz like flies about human souls;
  You marked the vice and the pride that lolls
In the pompous purple of Christly creeds;
  You saw how life, in its long advance,
  Is slave to satiric circumstance;
You shared all loftiest want and woe,
    Gentleman Jo! Gentleman Jo!

No sounding cant could your faith convince
  To adore some God whom the people plan
  In the poor similitude of a man,
A little larger than priest or prince.

That impious piety vexed you well
   Which says of God, the unthinkable,
He is or He is not thus and so,
     Gentleman Jo! Gentleman Jo!

What wonder you dropt off tired, my friend,
   From the brutelike human rush for gain?
   What wonder that your true heart and brain
Turned very weary before the end? . . .
   Till your spirit's beautiful steadfast light
   Flickered in death's cold wind, one night,
As I watched your last breath weakly go,
     Gentleman Jo! Gentleman Jo!

You are vanished away in shadow vast,
   Yet your loss has left to me moments dear
   When the stars of memory steal out clear,
To tremble in twilights of the past!
   The world, although she owed you a crown
   Of lordliest laurel, smote you down!
And all she lost she shall never know,
     Gentleman Jo! Gentleman Jo!

PIPES AND BEER.

BEFORE I was famous I used to sit
   In a dull old underground room I knew,
And sip cheap beer, and be glad for it,
   With a wild Bohemian friend or two.

And oh, it was joy to loiter thus,
   At peace in the heart of the city's stir,
Entombed, while life hurried over us,
   In our lazy bacchanal sepulchre.

There was artist George, with the blond Greek head,
   And the startling creeds, and the loose cravat;
There was splenetic journalistic Fred,
   Of the sharp retort and the shabby hat;

There was dreamy Frank, of the lounging gait,
   Who lived on nothing a year, or less,
And always meant to be something great,
   But only meant, and smoked to excess;

And last myself, whom their funny sneers
   Annoyed no whit as they laughed and said,
' I listened to all their grand ideas
   And wrote them out for my daily bread.'

The Teuton beer-bibbers came and went,
   Night after night, and stared, good folk,
At our table, noisy with argument,
   And our chronic aureoles of smoke.

And oh, my life! but we all loved well
    The talk, free, fearless, keen, profound,
The rockets of wit that flashed and fell
    In that dull old tavern underground! . . .

But there came a change in my days at last,
    And fortune forgot to starve and stint,
And the people chose to admire aghast
    The book I had eaten dirt to print.

And new friends gathered about me, then,
    New voices summoned me there and here;
The world went down in my dingy den,
    And drew me forth from the pipes and beer.

I took the stamp of my altered lot,
    As the sands of the certain seasons ran,
And slowly, whether I would or not,
    I felt myself growing a gentleman.

But now and then I would break the thrall,
    I would yield to a pang of dumb regret,
And steal to join them, and find them all,
    With the amber wassail near them yet.

Find, and join them, and try to seem
    A fourth for the old queer merry three,
With my fame as much of a yearning dream
    As my morrow's dinner was wont to be.

But the wit would lag, and the mirth would lack,
    And the god of jollity hear no call,
And the prosperous broadcloth on my back
    Hung over their spirits like a pall!

It was not that they failed, each one, to try
    Their warmth of welcome to speak and show;
I should just have risen and said good-bye,
    With a haughty look, had they served me so.

It was rather that each would seem, instead,
    With not one vestige of spleen or pride,
Across a chasm of change to spread
    His greeting hands to the further side.

And our gladdest words rang strange and cold,
    Like the echoes of other long-lost words;
And the nights were no more the nights of old
    Than Spring would be Spring without the birds!

So they waned and waned, these visits of mine,
    Till I married the heiress, ending here.
For if caste approves the cigars and wine,
    She must frown perforce upon pipes and beer.

And now 'tis years since I saw these men,
    Years since I knew them living yet.
And of this alone I am sure, since then—
    That none has gained what he toiled to get.

For I keep strict watch on the world of art,
    And George, with his wide rich-dowered brain!
His fervent fancy, his ardent heart,
    Though he greatly toiled, has toiled in vain.

And Fred, for all he may sparkle bright
    In caustic column, in clever quip,
Of a truth must still be hiding his light
    Beneath the bushel of journalship.

And dreamy Frank must be dreaming still,
   Lounging through life, if yet alive,
Smoking his vast preposterous fill,
   Lounging, smoking, striving to strive.

And I, the fourth in that old queer throng,
   Fourth and least, as my soul avows, —
I alone have been counted strong,
   I alone have the laurelled brows!

Well, and what has it all been worth?
   May not my soul to my soul confess
That "succeeding," here upon earth,
   Does not alway assume success?

I would cast, and gladly, from this gray head
   Its crown, to regain one sweet lost year
With artist George, with splenetic Fred,
   With dreamy Frank, with the pipes and beer!

TO AN OLD STREET-LAMP.

I WATCH thee now, with meditative mood,
   In the old street, noiseless under midnight's spell,
Whereof through many a midnight hast thou stood,
   Poor flickering lamp, the yellow sentinel.
Thine humble flame no rivalry invites;
   More than thyself thou dost not care to seem;
Thou art not of the world's most shining lights,
   Yet what thou art is of benignant beam!

TO AN OLD STREET-LAMP.

Harsh gusts that haughtiest waves have reared and
    rocked,
  Sweeping the untraversed street with lonely roar,
Have paused amid their savage speed and knocked
  With frigid knuckles at thy glassy door.
Half draped in snow-drift thou hast burned obscure:
  Innumerous rain-streaks thy dull panes have crost,
And cold has vestured thine uncouth contour
  In pale fantastic filigrees of frost!

And ah, the uncounted faces thou hast lit,
  Seen but by fleeting intervals before
Each into distance and the dark would flit,
  Some to return again, and some no more!
The moneyed autocrat; the beggar meek;
  The shambling rag-pick, half a man for mud;
The exhausted work-girl, on whose wasting cheek
  Blooms the white flower that drinks the toiler's
    blood!

The young bride, near her lord, all life at rest;
  The expectant lover, speeding to his tryst;
The wearied house-drudge, with her babe at breast,
  And forehead purpled from a brutish fist;
The ruminant poet, with his rusty coat;
  The thief that shoots to covert in hot flight;
The reveller, flinging from audacious throat
  A reckless dithyramb on the startled night!

Theirs hast thou seen, and many another's face,
  Since this thy special flame was called by fate
To illume, from its unclassic biding-place,
  These stolid pavements' monochrome of slate.

For now the ladder that first scaled thine height
    Is fallen, perchance, to utter rot and rust,
And doubtless the first hand that gave thee light
    Knows now the unending quietude of dust!

Hast thou not sometimes heard a bacchanal tongue
    Pay thee sad slanders, worth no honest heed,
While arms about thy rigid pillar clung
    With the fierce friendship of a friend in need?
Yet then, I doubt not, thou wert calm no less,
    Though named unstable in delirious strain,
Too proudly conscious of thy steadfastness
    For any answer but a dumb disdain!

Patient and unpretentious, with the sweet
    Desire alike to live for low and high,
Shine on, old lamp, within the shadowy street
    Where fortune hath ordained thy lot to lie!
And mayst thou fade, when time at last shall tell
    The gaseous ardor from thy pipe to cease,
Like one that having done his duty well
    Sinks to oblivion with a brow of peace!

A BARNYARD ECLOGUE.

GOOD neighbor mine, can you endure
   To look on man in miniature?
I keep no magic mirror hid,
(As the ancient Cagliostros did)
Unveiling it for one to see
Humanity in epitome.
Or, if at all with such I deal,
'Tis only that my powers reveal
Those fleet fantastic shapes which pass
O'er caricature's cracked looking-glass?

Now do you love your race too well
To admit the comic parallel
That lies between ourselves and this
Ornithologic metropolis,
Which near us clucks and struts and thrives, —
Four hundred appetizing lives?
That fowl in whose tail's ebon sweep
Rich emerald lustres love to sleep,
Who deems his top-knot, black as tar,
To have doubtless crowned him barnyard czar,
Or heir presumptive, beyond all ban,
To El Dorados of golden bran —
Search Europe, and you shall not see
Such an aristocrat as he!

But there are those before whose brow
Even this black Marmion must bow,

Though ill can brook his haughty eye
Precedence from such low *canaille*.
Look yonder, where the lord doth stand
Of all this polygamic land, —
The sultan, caliph, Brigham Young
Of the abject throngs he rules among;
Or, as we call, in homelier talk,
His Highness — Cock of All the Walk!
What boots it in one's veins to hold
A royal current, rare and old —
Be prince by right of head-tuft, legs,
Through ancestries of blameless eggs,
When some vile upstart crows with zeal
On heights no vulgar claw should feel,
Rearing a head that seems to glow
With Communism's red overflow?
Alas! the tribes are few on earth
Where brute force may not level birth!
These feathered Bourbons do but serve
To show the usurper's hardy nerve,
And prove by their own bitter smarts
Even barnyards may have Bonapartes!

Mark with what grave maternal pride
This patient hen, her chicks at side,
Moves like a dame of proud degree,
Each chick a sort of live *pe-wee*,
Filling with sound that scarce knows hush
Its biped ball of tawny plush.
Ill could we find in human mood
More motherly solicitude,
Or the intense devotion match
Of that same strenuous awkward scratch,

Whose good results, whate'er they be,
Her offspring seize in hot sortie,
While o'er them, softly wishing luck,
Sounds her self-abnegating *cluck*.
Ah, what rich burlesque may we trace
On the "fat, fair and forty" race,
In this majestic hen, this gray
Cornelia of a latter day,
Showing, with all their plaintive din,
Her downy Gracchi, six times twin!
What eye but plainly finds in her,
The yard's bucolic dowager,
A life that stands (no common boon!)
At chickenhood's mellow afternoon?
Her figure, as one promptly sees,
Attains *embonpoint's* ampler ease,
From early indiscretions born
(Girls will be girls) in granary-corn ;
And with her matron mien we find
A sad austerity entwined —
Something that tells us, at a glance,
She has outlived her first romance,
And buried young love's dream, may be,
In some long-eaten fricassee !

Notice that plain ill-favored cock,
Commonplace, of indifferent stock.
Thus far about his earthly lot
The least delights have gathered not.
Always, through some harsh whim of fate's,
A neighbor beak beside him waits,

Ready to seize, ere he can guess,
The yellow corn-grain of success.
And much change hath he seen withal,
Since first he served as fortune's ball :
The low turned high, the high made low
By flashy plume and pompous crow;
Discord and pecking; rise and fall,
Now social, now political ;
Governments trembling with the shock
Of some great head brought to the block ;
Those reigns of terror that we men
Rouse in the barnyard now and then,
Robespierres, Dantons setting free
When company drops in to tea,
And eating broiled, with no regrets,
Gallinaceous Marie Antoinettes !
Such change and more hath passed him by,
Met now with philosophic eye,
Since he at last in heart has come
To observe events in Roosterdom
With ripened wisdom's critic view,
As so much . . . cockadoodledoo !

Ah, friend, for hours my speech might brood
O'er many an odd similitude,
And let, while murmuring careless things,
Analogy fly with fancy's wings.
We all know well, who know aright,
Some foolish fowls will sometimes fight ;
But far too rudely have I rent
The apparent veil of sweet content

That wraps with such idyllic charm
These simple gypsies of the farm.
Best in their harmless joys believe,
Nor brush, with too bold sweep of sleeve,
From fruit so seeming-fresh of hue
The illusive damask of its dew!
If human greed, spite, envy stirs
These gentle wayside foragers,
(Captives that never need a guard,
Meek tentless Bedouins of the yard)
Why, best that we should shirk intact
The disenchanting realm of fact,
Skeptic as though some lip to-day
To our incredulous ear should say:
" In yonder garden's glimmering close,
The lily wrangles with the rose."

Ah, that recalls, before you go,
The new grand rose I was to show;
(Follow this narrow footpath, please,
Down-hill beyond the cedar-trees).
A royal rose, good neighbor mine,
Large, deep and gold as Rhenish wine!

III.

SONNETS.

ART.

I SAW in dreams a shape of mightiest mold,
   Wrought from stern bronze and towering in mid-
     air;
   A grand similitude of some goddess, fair
With a beauty radiant yet supremely cold.
She seemed invisible distance to behold,
   Nor ever drooped her languorous look to where,
   Down-broadening from her pedestal, a stair
Of ample depth imperially outrolled.

And on these haughty steps, crouched suppliantwise,
   I saw, at differing intervals apart,
     Sad men who seemed to adore, lament, entreat;
And one, a poet, with anguish in his eyes,
   Tore from a wound his own red quivering heart
     And flung it against the statue's brazen feet!

GENIUS.

As haughty Artemis, virgin without stain,
   Once drooped, in passionate grace, her mouth's warm flower
To young Endymion's lips amid the bower
Where tired on shady turf the boy had lain,
Even thus, at moments rare, some youth will gain
   The kiss of another goddess, great in power, —
   And all his spirit is troubled, from that hour,
Perpetually by sweet unearthly pain!

Either among the future's visitant dreams,
   Pale Sculpture's calm ideals his soul entrance,
     Or round him Painting's heavens of color rise,
Or through his thought strange eloquent Music streams,
   Or Poesy lures him with her velvet glance
     And white limbs lovelier than the Lorelei's!

SLEEP.

(For a Picture.)

A YELLOW sunset, soft and dreamy of dye,
   Met sharply by black fluctuant lines of grass;
A river, glimmering like illumined glass,
And narrowing till it ends in distant sky;
Pale scattered pools of luminous rain, that lie
   In shadowy amplitudes of green morass;
   A crescent that the old moon, as moments pass,
Has turned to a silver acorn hung on high!

Now through this melancholy and silent land
   Sleep walks, diaphanous-vestured, vaguely fair.
Within her vaporous robe and one dim hand
   Much asphodel and lotus doth she bear,
Going lovely and low-lidded, with a band
   Of dull-red poppies amid her dull-gold hair!

TO ———.

(On receiving a Volume of his Poems.)

IT is not only that your poesy shows
   Exquisite elegance and daintiest care,
  But through its melody, as a grace more rare,
The protean soul of Nature moves and glows.
Now gayly, like some radiant brook, it flows,
   Now with a violet's fragrance perfumes air,
   And now its tropic luxury seems to wear
The balmy crimson of an opening rose!

I think that if your kindlier fate had been
   To have lived when lover-minstrels were not mute,
     You might have sung, reclined at languorous ease,
Amid some tapestried chamber's gold and green,
   To some fair damosel, on some ribboned lute,
     Such delicate and delicious songs as these!

THE CITY.

WHEN night is on the city and silence reigns,
    How all its dark tranquillity, bathed in sleep,
Is like that quietude of the ocean's deep
Remotely above whose realm the surge complains!
For even as monsters that o'er weird domains
    Of cold subaqueous dimness dart and creep,
    Within the vague metropolis wakeful keep
Those hideous vices that its heart retains!

In fancy I watch black crimes like sea-growths loom;
    In fancy I view large hopes, once fair and whole,
        Grown wrecks where memory's mosses now unfurl.
Yet here and there, amid the encircling gloom,
    I know that some serene exceptional soul
        Dwells in its lovely purity, like a pearl!

KINDLINESS.

FAR more than many a lawless life may guess,
    Pure kindliness hath a spell they only know
    Whose hearts, however assailed by care and woe,
Have cause its sweet talismanic worth to bless!
It looks at first a power of feeble stress,
    Yet fights with dauntless fortitude blow for blow,
    Until some towering human fault lies low,
Beneath this delicate spell of kindliness!

Thus, when the radiant spear of Perseus leapt
    Against that wallowing bulk of scaly hide,
        It seemed like a reed by contrast, and as firm...
But when with gradual surge the sea had crept
    About Andromeda's rock, its falling tide
        Bore slowly off the monstrous, massacred worm!

COMMONPLACES.

TROUBLED in spirit at the unvaried ways
    Wherewith perpetually I seemed to view,
In regular and familiar retinue,
Coming and going, the processional days,
I yearned to mark with many a novel phase
    This round of dull monotonies that I knew,
    And treat life's commonplaces, dreary of hue,
As phantoms that the intellect sternly lays!

But wheresoe'er my wandering feet might be,
    Like some persistent word that memory saith,
Or like a ship's own shadow on wastes of sea,
    Or the very wind's inevitable breath,
I found, among all changes, following me
    The dark ubiquitous commonplace of death!

CITY WINDOWS.

THROUGH many an evening, while my spirit gains,
    Amid the populous city's ebb and flow,
A keener sense of solitude than they know
Who dwell on desolate hills or houseless plains,
I roam long streets where dubious dimness reigns,
    Where bright inscrutable windows calmly glow,
    And with mysterious pleasure, as I go,
Shape weird conjectures from the illumined panes!

In yonder room two amorous hearts may thrill;
    Some fiery quarrel, here, may grow apace;
There may some vigilant mother, pale and still,
    Bend in deep agony o'er a wasting face;
And here a murderess by some bed may spill
    The deadly colorless drop that leaves no trace!

A THISTLE.

O ROSEATE thistle, blooming by a rock,
    With fragrant silkiness in prickly thrall,
How darkly, while I watch you, does it fall
That o'er me such disconsolate fancies flock?
I see calamitous battles, feel the shock
    Of treachery and intrigue, revolt and brawl;
    I see (oh, saddest picture of them all!)
Pale Mary cowering by the ghastly block!

Ah, wherefore think such bitter thoughts as these,
    While sweet auroral freshness charms and cheers?
Why mar the morning's brilliance and its breeze
    With weary memories of those crimeful years?
    Why tell this poor flower in what blood and tears
They have bathed its Scottish kindred overseas!

MAPLES.

AMID this maple-avenue, on the brow
   Of this cool hill, while summer suns were bold,
No gaudier coloring could I then behold
Than the deep green of many a breezy bough;
But up the foliaged vista gazing now,
Where Autumn's halcyon brilliancies unfold
And opulent scarlet blends with dazzling gold,
I feel my wandering fancy dream of how,
In some old haughty city, centuries since,
Before the coming of some conqueror-prince
Back from famed fights with all his war-worn bands,
While jubilant bells in tower and steeple swung,
Down over sculptured balconies were hung
Great gorgeous tapestries out of Eastern lands!

A COBWEB.

LOVER devout of many a lonely place,
   Mute gossamer guest of dimness and repose,
  As loyally as lily or balmy rose
Obey the sunshine, does your delicate lace
Hang sombre filaments where the stealthy pace
   Of time's disfeaturing footstep vaguely goes, —
  From shelves that bear old ponderous folios,
To some poor yellowing portrait's dusty face!

Yet though in solemn nooks you rightly reign,
  Here, woven across the green of this fresh vine,
    The dignity of your wonted state you lose;
For now the halcyon morning on your skein,
  As though to merrily challenge its dark sign,
    Strings the warm splendors of her jewelling dews!

AN OCTOBER DAY.

THE emergent sun looks forth on sparkling grass,
    Filmed with the frost's pale gossamer of snow.
And now long resonant breezes wake and blow
The empurpled mists from meadow and morass.
The withering aster shivers ; dry leaves pass ;
Red sumachs burn ; the yellowing birches glow ;
And on the elastic air, in many a mass,
Rolling through pale-blue heaven, the great clouds go !

In the afternoon all windy sounds are still :
From wooded ways the cricket's chirp takes flight,
And the dreamy Autumn hours lapse on until . . .
See ! the sweet evening-star, that night by night
Drops luminous, like an ever-falling tear,
Down dying twilights of the dying year !

A WILLOW-TREE.

PALE sorrower, in whose listless grace one sees
    Not any shadow of joy while summer beams,
Looking, as all your foliage earthward streams,
The inconsolable Niobe of trees,
For me, if some appropriate mood shall please
    To have led me where your leafy languor gleams,
    Then through my heart, a band of glimmering dreams,
Float these, or lovelier memories than these :

A white shape, framed in jealous passion's gloom,
    Meek Desdemona doth her sad song raise ;
Or mad Ophelia, just before her doom,
    Hangs on your treacherous branch her wildwood sprays ;
Or yet, this hour, you shade De Musset's tomb,
    Among the sculpturings of old Père la Chaise !

THISTLEDOWN.

THROUGH summer's gradual death, how sweet a sight
   The flowering thistle's tardy gleam appears,
   Her thorny boughs like intricate chandeliers
When lit for festival with soft rosy light!
Yet closelier watching her, to left and right
   You see the odorous beauty that she rears
   Girt on all sides with countless emerald spears,
Eager the invading hand to pierce or smite!

But when the autumnal trees in ruin glow,
You meet her white ghost wandering to and fro
   Aerially upon the fitful blast,
As though the spirit of this proud blossom came
To haunt the world in expiatory shame,
   Repentant of her cold imperious past!

FABRICS.

I. VELVET.

HERE fittingly is the one most regal dress,
    For in the manner its full round folds divide
  We see superb calm and imperial pride
With soft alluring luxury acquiesce.
Now we behold it utterly lustreless,
    Now mellow glimmerings in its depths abide,
    Where masses of rich varying shadow hide,
Close-wedded to its sumptuous heaviness.

Always it shows me some traditional scene
    Of thrones, ambassadors and the pomp of rule,
        Great marriages, princely promises held cheap,
The pampered favorite, the neglected queen,
    The reckless insolence of the gaudy fool,
        The fawning courtier, and the assassin's leap!

II. SATIN.

NO moonlit pool is lovelier than the glow
    Of this bright sensitive texture, nor the sheen
On sunny wings that wandering sea-birds preen;
And sweet, of all fair draperies that I know,
To mark the smooth tranquillity of its flow,
    Where shades of tremulous dimness intervene,
    Shine out with mutable splendors, mild, serene,
In some voluminous raiment white as snow.

For then I feel impetuous fancy drawn
    Forth at some faint and half-mysterious call,
        Even like a bird that breaks from clasping bars;
And lighted vaguely by the Italian dawn,
    I see rash Romeo scale the garden-wall,
        While Juliet dreams below the dying stars!

III. BROCADE.

WHEN, in the festal glory of grand events,
    This pale-flowered silk some stately form ensheathes,
Wrought intricately with pearly sprays and wreaths,
Arabesques and scrolls and leaflike ornaments,
What memories of old majesties intense
    To the present its elaborate woof bequeathes,
    Whose very rustle and sweep augustly breathes
Of leisure and wealth and grave magnificence.

For when I watch it, amber, yellow or rose,
    As though some delicate wand were waved in air
    By some invisible wondersmith, I gaze
On courtly gentlemen with embroidered hose
    And radiant ladies with high powdered hair,
    Stepping through minuets in colonial days!

THE OLD MIRROR.

IN yonder homestead, wreathed with bounteous vines,
   A lonely woman dwells, whose wandering feet
     Pause often amid one chamber's calm retreat,
Where an old mirror from its quaint frame shines.
And here, soft-wrought in memory's vague designs,
   Dim semblances her wistful gaze will greet
     Of lost ones that in thrall phantasmally sweet
The mirror's luminous quietude enshrines.

But unto her these dubious forms that pass
   With shadowy majesty or dreamy grace,
     Wear nothing of ghostliness in mien or guise.
The only ghost that haunts this glimmering glass
   Carries the sad reality in its face
     Of her own haggard cheeks and desolate eyes!

EARTHQUAKE.

A GIANT of awful strength, he dumbly lies
    Far-prisoned among the solemn deeps of earth;
The sinewy grandeurs of his captive girth, —
His great-thewed breast, colossally-molded thighs,
And arms thick-roped with muscle of mighty size,
    Repose in a slumber where no dream gives birth
    For months, even years, to any grief or mirth;
A slumber of tranquil lips, calm-lidded eyes!

Yet sometimes to his spirit a dream will creep
    Of the old glad past when clothed in dauntless pride
        He walked the world, unchained by tyrannous powers;
And then, while he tosses restlessly in sleep,
    Dark terrible graves for living shapes yawn wide,
        Or a city shrieks among her tottering towers!

TO F. S. S.

> "C'était un démon se tordant sous un ange,
> Un enfer sous un ciel."
> THÉOPHILE GAUTIER.

SEEING thy face, with all thy fluctuant hair
   Falling in dull-gold opulence from thy brow,
Watching thy light-blue eyes, now fired or now
Laughterful, or now dim as with despair,
I wonder, friend, that it should be God's care
To have made at all, what matter when or how,
A being so sadly, desolately rare,
So beautifully incomplete as thou!

O rank black pool, with one star's imaged form!
O sweet rich-hearted rose, with rot at core!
O summer heaven, half purpled by stern storm!
O lily, with one white leaf dipt in gore!
O angel-shape, whereover curves and clings
The awful imminence of a devil's wings!

MEDUSA.

(For a Picture.)

A FACE in whose voluptuous bloom there lies
   Olympian faultlessness of mold and hue ;
  Lips that a god were worthy alone to woo ;
Round chin, and nostrils curved in the old Greek wise.
But there is no clear pallor of arctic skies,
   Fathom on crystal fathom of livid blue,
   So bleakly cold that one might liken it to
The pitiless icy splendors of her eyes !

Her bound hair, colored lovelier than the sweet
Rich halcyon yellow of tall harvest wheat,
   Over chaste brows a glimmering tumult sheds ;
But through the abundance of its warm soft gold,
Coils of lean horror peer from many a fold,
   With sharp tongues flickering in flat clammy heads !

ANTIPODES.

I. POE.

HE loved all shadowy spots, all seasons drear;
    All ways of darkness lured his ghastly whim;
  Strange fellowships he held with goblins grim,
At whose demoniac eyes he felt no fear.
On midnights through dense darkness he would peer,
    To watch the pale ghoul feed, by tombstones dim.
  The appalling forms of phantoms walked with him,
And murder breathed its red guilt in his ear!

By desolate paths of dream, where fancy's owl
    Sent long lugubrious hoots through sombre air,
Amid thought's gloomiest caves he went to prowl,
    And met delirium in her awful lair,
And mingled with cold shapes that writhe or scowl,
    Serpents of horror, black bats of despair!

II. WHITTIER.

FRESH as on breezy seas the ascendant day,
   And bright as on thick dew its radiant trace ;
Pure as the smile on some babe's dreaming face ;
Hopeful as meadows at the breath of May,
One loftiest aim his melodies obey,
   Like dawnward larks in roseate deeps of space —
While that large reverent love for all his race
Makes him a man in manhood's lordlier way !

His words like pearls are luminous yet strong ;
   His duteous thought ennobles while it calms ;
We seem to have felt the falling, in his song,
   Of benedictions and of sacred balms ;
To have seen the aureoled angels group and throng
   In heavenly valleylands, by shining palms !

CAMEOS.

I. THACKERAY.

WITH satire's poignant spear he loved to fight,
    And flocks of scampering falsehoods to disband,
    So sinewy were the savage blows he planned,
So sweeping yet so accurate his keen sight!
Than he no man more loyally loved the right,
    No man could wrong more valiantly withstand,
    Who shook the old human web with such fierce hand
That half fraud's ambushed vermin swarmed to light!

How forcefully could he paint the proud grandee;
    The skilled adventuress, with her game sly-played;
    The toadying snob, in triple brass arrayed;
The dissolute fop; the callous debauchee;
    And dowagers, in rouge, feathers and brocade,
Sneering at life across their cards and tea!

II. DICKENS.

AS one who flings large hospitable doors
    Wide to a world of masquers whom he has bade
Sweep hurrying onward with their paces mad,
And gaily flood the vacant chamber-floors,
Even so with him about whose form in scores
    Humanity's eager passions, blithe or sad,
    Rush revelling, and however strangely clad,
Are still the old rascals, bigots, fools and bores!

Ah! what a riotous witch-dance they prolong
    Of avarice, hatred, hope, revenge, despair!
How right flies timorous from the clutch of wrong!
    How pleasure and ease take hands with toil and care!
    While humor, that wild harlequin, here and there
Dashes in spangled somersaults through the throng!

III. KEATS.

IT fell, in youthful hours, that he should stray
   To some enchanted garden's magic gate,
   And being elect that he should pass elate
Where long parterres of blossoming splendor lay.
But while he gathered many a fragrant spray,
   In passionate rapture and in wonder great,
   Death, gliding up to him with eyes like fate
And cold implacable hand, led him away!

Yet later, lingering briefly among men,
   He dropt before the world's feet those few flowers
     Whose color and odor brave all blight of years,
And the rare radiance of whose bloom, since then,
   Pathos, their sweet attendant, ever dowers
     With the soft silver dews of pitying tears!

IV. DUMAS, *PÈRE.*

BORN heir-presumptive to Boccaccio's bays,
    What generous genial art this man possessed,
Pillaging history's mighty treasure-chest,
Loving the most her most adventurous days;
Painting, in such adroit and happy phrase,
    King, priest, cavalier, the jester with his jest,
    Or D'Artagnan, big Porthos and the rest,
Who fought so valorously for Louis Treize!

No morbid analyst, healthful, honest, bland,
    How he adored all perilous deeds and wild!
Romance's monarch, story-teller grand,
    How long he made, by halcyon spells beguiled,
Great haughty France, with head upon her hand,
    Crouch at his feet and listen like a child!

V. HANS CHRISTIAN ANDERSEN.

NOW that we know him dead, conjecture brings
   The marvelling fancies it can ill control ;
   We picture in some last fair dreamy goal
Him round whose name such dreamy influence clings.
In some strange land that teems with butterfly-wings,
   Flower-cradled fairies, elf-shapes grimly droll,
   We see his calm and incontaminate soul
Walk with delight amid miraculous things !

And yet, although his dear Valhalla lies
   At happiest distance from all earthly harms,
   We are sure he will not love its choicest charms
Unless, however opulent, these comprise
Children, with shining hair, with limpid eyes,
   To enwreathe him in their balmy rosy arms !

VI. HERBERT SPENCER.

A SPACIOUS-BRAINED arch-enemy of lies,
   For years he has followed, with sure pace and
      fleet,
The stainless robe and radiant-sandalled feet
That truth makes vaguely visible as she flies.
For years he has searched, with undiscouraged eyes,
   Deep at the roots of life, eager to meet
   One law beneath whose sovereignty complete
Each vast and fateful century dawns or dies!

His intellect is a palace, on whose walls
   Great rich historic frescoes may be seen,
   And where, in matron dignity of mien,
Meeting perpetually amid its halls
Messages from victorious generals,
   Calm Science walks, like some majestic queen!

VII. GUSTAVE DORÉ.

HOW rare the audacious spirit that invokes
    These shadowy grandeurs, and can bid appear
    All horror's genii, awful and austere,
And paint infinity with a few strong strokes!
That steals where mortal suffering writhes and chokes,
    Where sorrow has wept her last hot heavy tear,
    And where, while moans of misery smite the ear,
Some great calamitous battle roars and smokes!

Now are we fain to applaud him, — and anon
    To shrink from power of such uncanny spell;
We tire of death's chill touch and visage wan;
    Of agony; of corruption's rank sick smell;
Of this strange soul that seems to have gazed upon
    Terrific things in the red heart of hell!

VIII. BAUDELAIRE.

O POET of such unique fantastic rhyme,
    Lover of some strange muse who bound her hair
  With poisonous myrtles, grown in no Greek air
But fostered of some feverous Gothic clime;
Degenerate god, half loathsome, half sublime,
    By what fatality wert thou led to fare
    Through haunts that all corruption's colors wear,
Through pestilent noisome paths of woe and crime?

For me thy poesy's morbid splendors wake
    A thought of how, in close miasmatic gloom,
Deep amid some toad-haunted humid brake
    That dark moss clothes or flexuous fern-leaves
        plume,
Some rank red fungus, dappled like a snake,
    Spots the black dampness with its clammy bloom!

Cambridge: Press of John Wilson & Son.

www.ingramcontent.com/pod-product-compliance
Lightning Source LLC
Chambersburg PA
CBHW020919230426
43666CB00008B/1499